POETICALLY TOGETHER

How never giving up
Brought us together

Greg and Kathy Weller

"Beautiful, honest, and transparent ... This is a poetic, unconventional tale of love ... and how God masterfully weaves a unique tapestry–us."
Peter Shurley, Pastor & Award-winning singer/songwriter

POETICALLY TOGETHER

HOW NEVER GIVING UP
BROUGHT US TOGETHER

BY GREG AND KATHY WELLER
(authors of Age of Peril)

There's Hope, even
in the long waiting...

Poetically Together: How never giving up brought us together by Greg & Kathy Weller
Copyright © 2022 by Greg & Kathy Weller
All Rights Reserved.
ISBN: 978-1-59755-699-6

Published by: ADVANTAGE BOOKS™ www.advbookstore.com

This book and parts thereof may not be reproduced in any form, stored in a retrieval system or transmitted in any form by any means (electronic, mechanical, photocopy, recording or otherwise) without prior written permission of the author, except as provided by United States of America copyright law.

All Scriptures within quotation marks are quoted from the Holy Bible King James Version, Public Domain.

Library of Congress Catalog Number: 2022946046

Names:	Weller, Greg, Author
	Weller, Kathy, Author
Title:	***Poetically Together: How never giving up brought us together***
	Greg & Kathy Weller
	Advantage Books, 2022
Identifiers:	ISBN (print): 9781597556996, (mobi, epub): 9781597557122, (hardcover): 9781597557207
Subjects:	Christian Life: Inspirational

First Printing October 2022
22 23 24 25 26 27   10 9 8 7 6 5 4 3 2 1

DEDICATION

We would like to thank Graeme & Jo Semple: firstly for journeying with Kathy for over thirty years, showing her what Christ's love looks like and exemplifying unconditional love; and secondly, for journeying with us throughout our relationship and in putting this book together.

Thank you for inspiring, encouraging and loving.

We love you greatly.

Kathy & Greg

Greg and Kathy Weller

Table of Contents

DEDICATION 5
INTRODUCTION 11

TWO SEPARATE SONGS

1: The Expectant One 1 15
2: The Expectant One 2 15
3: Kathy's Big Birthday 16
4: Greg Husk 17
5: Kathy–Such Pressure To Compromise 18
6: Greg–Eharmony Subscription Begins 18
7: Greg–Costs Paid 19
8: Kathy–Forty-Four And Depressed 20
9: Greg At The Hospital–On The Night Of Mum's Fall 21
10: Greg–Mum's Funeral 22
11: Greg–After Mum's Death 22
12: Kathy At 45–Farm And Farmer 24
13: Greg–Too Heavy After Mum's Passing 25
14: Greg–Powerless Alone 26
15: Kathy's Song Of Aloneness 27
16: Kathy—The Lottery And The Lie 30
17: Greg–A New Direction 31
18: Kathy–Eharmony Scam 31
19: Kathy–No Compromise 34
20: Greg Surveys The Future 35
21: Kathy–Why Won't Eharmony Deliver? 35
22: Greg–The Right Priorities 36

HEARING A NEW SONG

23: Kathy–Counsellor At Youth Camp 39
24: Kathy Sends A Wink To Greg 39
25: Greg Looks Back 40
26: Kathy–Words 41
27: Kathy's Song 42
28: Kathy–Getting To Know Greg 43

29: Kathy And Greg–Longing To Serve God Together 45
30: Kathy Recalls An Old Promise 45

THE DUET BEGINS
31: The Two Sing Together 51
32: Kathy's Friends Urge A Checking That Greg Is On The Level 51
33: The Two Thrill Together 52
34: The Two: "Will I Love You More Than My Right To Be Right?" 52
35: Kathy Hears Her Friends 54
36: Greg Receives The Request Whilst Walking 55
37: Greg Leaves The Physio, Tired 56
38: Greg And The Quirky Photo 57
39: Kathy Views The Photos 58
40: Kathy Writes 58
41: Greg Stands In Peril 59
42: Kathy Re-Evaluates Her Judgment Of The Photos 60
43: Greg's Internet And Eharmony Are Down 60
44: The Two Make Their First Phone Call 61
45: The Two Resolve To Always Allow Themselves To Self-Evaluate & Change 62
46: Greg Prepares For His Driving Test 64
47: Greg And The Driving Test 64
48: Greg Rings Kathy And Tells Her Of Changed Plans 66
49: Greg Reads The Email About Kathy Coming To His Town 67
50: At The Restaurant 67
51: Greg Reflects 69
52: Greg Makes His Plans 70
53: The Two–After <u>That</u> Weekend 70
54: Greg Arranges His First Car Trip To The Coast 78
55: Greg And The Early Morning Wait 79
56: Greg Rejoices 80
57: Kathy Rejoices 80
58: The Two On The Night Sands 81
59: Melody Maker 86
60: Greg Is Amazed 87
61: The Secret 88
62: Kathy Reflects 88
63: Greg's Nervous 4am Wait For Kathy For A Beach Walk 89

64: Greg, In Fear Of Rejection, Going Inwards 90
65: The Two, Among The Aunts, Dance Inside 91
66: The Two Experiment In Trust 93
67: Hot Longing Nights 93
68: The Two Do Ikea 95
69: Greg Revels In His Woman 98
70: Greg Asks Kathy's Dad For Permission 98
71: Kathy's Love 100

MELODY RUSHES TO CRESCENDO
72: Greg Is Nervous About How Serious It Is Getting 105
73: The Two Do Thai 106
74: The Two Seek To Communicate And Change 108
75: The Two Seek Their Goals 109
76: The Gondola 110
77: Kathy Thrills 113
78: Greg Has Jittery Nerves About Their Future Together 113
79: Kathy Knows Unknowing 114
80: Greg Reflects On Kathy's Sore Back 117
81: Kathy Responds 117
82: The Two Gift A Friend 117
83: The Hours 119
84: Greg Commits Without Knowing The Futurefall 119
85: The Two Search And Find 120
86: Greg Resolves His Actions 121
87: Kathy Rejoices 121
88: The Two Do The Comedy Club 121
89: Greg Struggles 125
90: The Two Want... 127
91: Kathy Struggles The Negative Predictions Of Their Future 128
92: Kathy Resolves 128
93: Greg Slides–And Recovers 129
94: Kathy Daydreams The Future 130
95: Greg Plans A Proposal 133
96: The Engagement Approaches 134
97: Changed Plans 134
98: The Asking 135

99: The Two Sing Together 139
100: Only God 139
101: Kathy Is Startled By The Question From Greg As To If She Loves Him 140
102: Love Song 141
103: Tears To Heaven 141
104: The Two Meet To Skype The Marriage Maker 143

HUMANS IN STACCATO AND BLUR

105: Staccato And Surprise 147
106: Staccato And Rush 148
107: The Finer Details 148
108: Shoot 149
109: Change And God 150
110: Buying A Bed Pt 1 150
111: Buying A Bed Pt 2 151
112: The Two Fear The Drift Apart 151
113: Ripples And Rushes 1 153
114: Kathy's Dream 157
115: Ripples And Rushes 2 158

APPENDIX ONE: THE THREE QUESTIONS 165

INTRODUCTION

This is the story of Kathy and Greg. They were in the world but they weren't of the world. They were a different shape. Where the world liked to talk about football and dresses, recipes and gossip about celebrities and wannabes, they liked deep talks and deep knowing of themselves and each other.

They were a different shape to the world. They lived their fairy tale, they moulded it and shaped it, discussed it and laughed at it. They weren't afraid to be wild and bushy and a little bit crazy in a hard world that had needless rules and protocols, and lots of frowns by others for those who didn't want to conform—and lots of frowns by others for those who wouldn't simply quietly value just the right trendy things and old old traditions.

This is their story—and they would like to offer you the chance that it become your story too.

TWO

SEPARATE

SONGS

Greg and Kathy Weller

Chapter 1
THE EXPECTANT ONE 1

Kathy stood surrounded by bridesmaids as they lifted the weaved gerbera garland and sat it gently on her purple hair.

She couldn't wait. She had been up all night chatting excitedly on the lounge and on the verandah and sprawled out in the bedroom with her older friend, the one whom she had cried with, sighed with, sobbed her longing to–because this man had taken more than 35 years to arrive in her life–and yet had taken less than four months to fall in love with her and laugh with her and propose to her and to look deeply deeply into her eyes with love.

It was almost time! Her wedding dress adorned her shoulders and arms and her excited face. The bridesmaids around her were dressed, little splashes of yellow on her happiness.

So excited so excited. So long to arrive, then like a whirlwind. Who would have thought after four months there would be a wedding! After four months, the future could so beautifully tug away all the past all of a sudden right now

She thought back...

Chapter 2
THE EXPECTANT ONE 2

He had run his race for years, had helped and cared for others. He had seen years of bad things, of sad things, years of wasted withering things. And then suddenly he had seen four months of beauty that had blossomed in his world's mud, a slender white rose that he rose to protect.

To be married soon! Obstacles had been vanquished, important people met and new relationships formed, treasure found and used and placed at her feet.

He loved her. Her feet entranced his hand, her hand entranced his lips. She his fine sex-hot lady–and he her prisoner of love, her hunter and collector, her ardent suitor and fervent admirer.

Only four months together–and soon to be married.

Year upon year of waiting–to find her. Energy evaporated in the family business, in meeting the needs of endless business students, in refining texts nightly, in remaining pure despite the hard hard longings, the unfulfilled longings that burnt down years and towns, the burning longings, and he running year upon year, running to be pure.

And now he had found her! Her soul that laughed in unison with him, their two voices that, with the same thought in mind, spoke all at once together the same words.

And her enchanting beauty. He would drift off to sleep thinking of her lips, her slender fingers, her purple hair her crown, her voice a symphony—just the best major melodic singing song.

How quick, how beautiful, how deep their romance—almost moving away all the long long painful years.

He thought back...

Chapter 3
KATHY'S BIG BIRTHDAY

Kathy smiled but—inside her the rain sobbed. Forty years old, surrounded by festivities because she was 40. And yet and yet...

The rain blattered against her. It ran down her, hit the ground and splashed up sorrow and grief and anger and not wanting to admit....

But it was no use. Storm clouds and floods and rage and helpless helpless longing...

"Life fleeing away from me. Too quick the years fall." And as her friends took her on an excited tour of their land, as they laughed and kidded and pulled each other's legs until merriment bubbled up, her soul rained its tears.

"I said once that if I was 40 alone, I would die. I would hold my soul and mouth tight till life faded from me, till I become emptiness, not this ready seed, till I become a dried-out thing picked up and carried away by the unfeeling gusty wind."

Alone... and she and they amazed at the bear that lurched across the way of their car, and they took photos and cheered and scared a little.

And then it was on to the next thing—the beautiful sky-blue lake that kissed the sky in the distance, kissed it with such feeling and love that they became alike—same colour, same calmness, same in spirit and in soul and in love

"I've tried, I've honestly tried," she thought. "I've lived pure, I've lived caring, I've lived smiling and helping others as THEY sob...

"Now who is there for me?"

"Who is HERE for me?"

and in her soul she looked around

"No one!" she thought

"No one!!"

And inside the floods overwhelmed all defenses.

Poetically Together

✳✳✳✳✳✳✳✳✳✳

Would that the night found our lips together–
And not me weeping,
My head upon this desert rock

Chapter 4
GREG HUSK

Greg stood outside the party. He was thirty-seven and at his friends' party–he loved and hated it

It's easier out here he thought...

Inside the festivities roared on. With merriment and music, the evening caroused.

"I don't know what to do in there, I've never known what to do."

"God is more true than my circumstances, and yet how is this humble hungry one, hungry for love, hungry for her lips, ever to find someone, to find her love, when all I have ever chosen is work, when early rejection leaves me only ever believing of friend and lover that 'I do so so believe you really don't ever want to see me.'

My mother terrified of my father's arms, hearing my teenage peers reject my friendship, the overcompensating till calluses scabbed the soul at twenty–and it became life, everyday life.

"O God, give me someone to teach me how to be social. I stand, a man longing to do and be right, but already just some primal husk, dry and dead. Yes, I go out to work, with books and forms, enthusiastic though torn, alone among comrades, more rejected than yesterday's fashion. I ride back, task complete, rich and replete, tired hands and eyes, but having never found my maiden, my princess of the high tower, my buxom beauty, my beauty of the entrancing eye. Whenever I thought I had found her, I was always pushed from her arms by a larger man, or while in reach of her hand found it suddenly jewelled by another's ring, or while daring to converse with another maiden to merely find that we loved and connected less than a careless breath... All this plays on my eye and hand and mouth even now.

"So I turn from the party and the surprisingly softer radio ballad, from the thump of cup and the chicken wings. Instead I stride with dry heart to even drier books and begin to write.

✳✳✳✳✳✳✳✳✳✳

The day after tomorrow
(After you are found)–
Victory that ends sorrow
Your "Hello"–the richest sound!

Chapter 5
KATHY–SUCH PRESSURE TO COMPROMISE

Day upon day pours down words.
Friend after relative after advisor after stranger.
"Forget your belief. Forget the furious fight to be pure. Forty is here, and the fury comes!"
My dearest friends each waltz away to a new man, forgetting all their first love, the teenage vow of purity and rightness and of firmness of faith.
Friends and relatives tell me of men, wild men, strong men, thieves and edges, drinking and shouting.
But who am I if not yours, oh God?
Who am I but someone who waits before you?
Who am I but someone who only ever wants to be your heartbeat, your heart's breath...
...your heart's breath to a starved world?

Chapter 6
GREG–EHARMONY SUBSCRIPTION BEGINS

The computer promised a year's subscription.
Pictures of matches spilled to the screen. Pictures of hopeful smiles playing the blush, the hair spilling–red or black, brown or blonde
My heart thudded. Undecided, but I had done it, I had signed.
eHarmony tumbled pictures of matches.
There might be matches, but yet...
Nerves in me made me notice the faults.
Terrified, I long for Adam and Eve in our skins, for I and her forgetting the world, forgetting the risks, forgetting the past and the too slowly gathering mist that makes all memories pleasant...

But the clock moves on! Time to work! Texts and pens and A4 await serious work. The clock hands find 7:30, and the night bundles to too short a possible deadline. I pray, sit down and begin the paper pile.

The fight will go on: deadlines will be conquered!

The screen stands quietly in the corner, promising...

And, as I sit down, I feel my heart nestle on the screen I had just left–my heart sits there near the nerves and fear.

****

> You are my love, my beautiful flower,
> You are my princess of the tower
> My heartfelt love, and yellow dancer
> You have poured sunshine into my soul
> And I am yours, in truth I'm yours

Chapter 7
GREG–COSTS PAID

All my characters paint my years...

New-born baby–and life brings me in through a twirling door of promises, of expenses paid, and futures assured.

Family care harbours an infant soul and keeps it safe

Romantic poverty crossed by futures and dreams.

A lost and hidden and worshipping family split by denominational fissures.

And I, smart and naive and faith-assured, no compromise even as time skitters by, I hold sanctuary and seek God's will alone (with or without tradition)

I police my person, break the sea for what's right, and yet still suddenly paralyse by fear burping momentarily into my night

I am a working worm with wings seeking to become butterfly, a slave of God whose passionate yearning for the world draws me to give myself away cheerfully as water to the ground. I am no conman, no snow blinder, no mirage shifter, no rose offerer to fade always before reaching hands. I am offerer and stayer, giver and bleeder, always lost and losing myself, seeking your health that God may pour health in you, always hovering like a waiter, so that you might walk to God.

My cradle and grave have come, will go, along with all heirlooms and monetary regrets. Even my ancestors with their momentary financial successes will acknowledge with me that there is a Man well worth all surrender, worth the total surrender

Chapter 8
KATHY–FORTY-FOUR AND DEPRESSED

There is black ice, and black wind that blows there.
I walk the icy road from church to rented home, never coming home in my soul.
There is no someday night, there is no man striding over the snow towards me, rose in his hand, and

>> he reaches me and his arms around
>> me and I pour into vividness, colour
>> and being

>> and
>> and
>> and there is only
>> the wind that howls at never finding future and hope
>> and the happy ending

There is only empty mental silver boxes prepared for the lover who never comes...

>> may never come

>> may never hold me to protect me from the chill wind and the
>>> chill years. I am
>>> forty-four and have
>>> come almost too far

>>> too far

>>> all too far to
>>>> find some male
>>>> angel's
>>>>> wing,

some miracle man
and
escape

Chapter 9
GREG AT THE HOSPITAL–ON THE NIGHT OF MUM'S FALL

I swallow horror. Nerves pace like sentries. Panic rolls and tumbles me a tighter porcupine.

I pluck out all my quills–so that I will remain defenceless and non-harming.

She has fallen. She reached for the curtain whilst clutching her wheelie-walker rollator. Her balance failed and down in a heap of frail bones and falls.

So we up, and to the hospital. Ambulance and me stepping forward to be her strength.

Waiting for results, and me plucking out all my quills, being quiet and supportive, being God's creature.

Me stilling myself to hold myself a calm, tight, alert creature. Pouring myself as water through a sieve, focusing to be only the sound of calm running water to the nerves of the one who bore me, my mother.

Duty is as Jesus did. The kenosis, the emptying, the giving myself away.

"Beloved this is how we know love:- that Jesus laid down his life for the brethren. And we also in the same way should lay down our lives for the brethren."

Lo I come. As water on a calm seaplain, I spread myself out. I spread my tense tense soul out.

" So as you can see," the doctor's voice calm and measured into the room," if you look at the x-ray, you can see the T8 vertebrae has had some slight crushing there. Due to osteoporosis it has had some moderate damage," but I stare at the chart and see vertebrae after vertebrae misshapen, see dozens of little fractures and then healings, so they run like melted wax

          like some twisted wax in some
          Salvador Dali dreaming

Leave the hospital consulting room. I and mum and family quietly file out.
They go home to their family.
I go home bearing up mum, quill-less and tight as iron.
Externally–I calm, and I reassure

I help her to bed
I lie me down too. I in my single bed too many rooms far from her.
I lie down foetal and quill-less.

Chapter 10
GREG–MUM'S FUNERAL

It is done
Age bleached brunette to heaven.
I watch her coffin. In many ways, I went first
What is there to rebuild?

...only <u>everything</u> that God would want.

Chapter 11
GREG–AFTER MUM'S DEATH

The house, her house
        my house
                only my house.

The morning, her honey and weetbix
        our camaraderie
               only my toast.
I am trying
  I am fighting
     this new stillness as I rise.

                Life of labour
                Life of vigour
                Life now being re-built.

Years upon years of pouring out. Pouring for her, pouring for the family-run Business College. If it would take me staying up to two am every night for three months, to take the time to write the notes and courses for one person–then it was done. Done, dusted, disposed of.

I have poured out my entire life.

Poured out for my church. Sunday school teacher–Saturday upon Saturday, 12 hours of preparation to be (with God's aid) the best Sunday School teacher I could–to be accurate, to be cool and relevant, to be only ever presenting what I had prayed through and soaked in prayer.

To be the church public address officer, to do the church microphones, the recording of the sermon onto cassette, the soundbooth tidying, the immediate soundbooth tidying after that of the Sunday School rooms, done for God, done for His people, done for love...

...and done for gladness that I was busy, and didn't need to face people.

When I was with a friend, I loved it, soaked it up, recharged, re-invigorated...

...but a group–three or more–I had learnt it was too painful.

At fifteen (all that time ago), I had conquered my little academic corner–straight A's for all subjects, academic prizes every year, on track to probably school dux. it was conquered...

And so, I had decided I could add social interaction back to my newly-accomplished one-and-a-half years of spending lunch hours in my Year 9 and most of my Year 10 in the library every lunch hour. I had already started to hang around–a little–and it had been good.

I saw them, twenty of them, in a large circle, and walked up to them to find them mocking me, rejecting me to each other–a large group of unanimity, it seemed to me–and I walked away, stunned.

Stunned had grown into shattered into concrete. It had happened in Grade 10, but it had grown and grown till fear of rejection had consumed all my interactions.

"Please, God," I had prayed, " let there be someone to be there, be someone to help me dare be Adam again, discover how to be a beginner again, discover how to talk and be, without fear, without interpreting every neutral glance as negative (for I'm sure I do that). Let there be someone who can teach me the skills of interacting that I had never known. Help me to learn the skills I should have learnt at 15 and 16 and 17 and 18, and through the years. And let me put aside the roles I have carried all these years to be who I am."

I had prayed that, then immediately I had plunged back into writing a new Business Course, had plunged into constitutional review for the church, had plunged into being a deacon, and only looked up from all the activity–occasionally–to find another 18 months had passed in a blur of paper and computers and red ticks.

I had become an orphan of my future, inept, lonely.

Now, now, I was at a new beginning, my future as wide as at 15, my future as enchained as I was at 16.

There were plans–in the past nine months since Mum had died, I had had my teeth fixed, an umbilical hernia and hiatus hernia unravelled, had enrolled to start at University in nine months time...

...but I was lonely

                      I needed a tribe–needed a woman.

I was lonely and terrified
    Ending the loneliness lay through terror
    Rejection, it seemed, stood arm-length away in all directions
It had been nine months, and I was losing steam.
    The world was becoming too big for me
    The world was becoming too indifferent for me
    I was starting to not want to find the world.
    The world was impossible outside
    The loneliness was impassable inside.

Chapter 12
KATHY AT 45–FARM AND FARMER

Hills like freckles around the homestead. The cattle breathed in country stillness and gave it back in still beauty.

He was my man, my farmer, my boyfriend and kissing one.

Sure, when we talked, words were of two worlds. When we dreamed, spotlights fell on separate scenes. When we worked, it was as mere co-workers, not lovers who pushed the edge together.

Come live with me, and be my wife
And we will all the house improve.
But I am woman, I am God's!
And deep deep down, I am not yours.

Kissing made our campfire, but soon it falls to ash.
Soon it fell to ash.

****

                  My unknown love,

I would push muscles to all limits
For you–
I would give you the world.

Chapter 13
GREG–TOO HEAVY AFTER MUM'S PASSING

I fold down

Determined before God, I straighten up
                                      but fold down

There is quietness here in this house.
                        It is full of maths and quietness

I stretch past the deep fears and fear of rejection
                                      but fold down

I am determined, but without energy

I will to will the good, to help others,
 to set the world's limits somewhat aside

I will to walk God's perfect way
                          but I fold down

There is so much effort
                          not to fold down

I sit up and work to exhaustion,
    tidying and sorting out all the clutter of years,
    all the papers,
    all the used-to-be's,
    all the energy in my body,
    then
Fall asleep

Without hope
Without energy

        I fold down.

He is so broken. He hurts in shadow corners. He flutters like a bird with a broken wing. Confidence has fled all his actions. He flies above barriers, but never past.

Chapter 14
GREG–POWERLESS ALONE

It's unfair. The world sings its own melody, runs its own race.
I had something cut out on my back, and was told to come home and bathe it each day. I dwell solitary at home, and there is no one to help...
The site sits at the exact point untouchable by arms and hands from any direction–I only had the shower to run on it, then let it air-dry... I had hoped that was enough–
But it became sorer and sorer–so I went to the hospital near me–and they ummed and finally said, "It's healing wrongly–we need to excoriate it.
"We need to scrape off the badly forming infected skin and make it a fresh wound so it can try to heal again properly."
So they scraped,
    and I who am solitary,
        returned home solitary–

Humiliated,
    angry, with
        bitterness of soul,

So solitary

    and mortal

      and

        alone.

Chapter 15
KATHY'S SONG OF ALONENESS

I, invited to so many weddings–yet so alone.

I, being made to sit at the reception table where no one knows anyone, because I always get everyone talking–

                                      and yet so alone.

I, being a bridesmaid and coming home late at night, being dropped off, and humiliatingly having to ask my friend to come in and unzip the dress that I couldn't undo alone, because there was no one at home, just me–

      alone.

My times at parties (Christmas parties, birthday parties): the grief causing so much pain, the loneliness no one could comprehend, the loneliness that made me want to end my life, because I am so

                                                    alone.

Friend after friend now getting married–even those I knew when they were born getting married, which rips at my heart and shreds me in pieces

Friend after friend having a baby … babies. I longed always to marry a man of God and have six babies … and yet there were none–just the grief and the physical ache in my body as a female so wanting children.

(My adopted brother and sister, whose nappies I used to change–now
        they're married,
        they're having children
    and every child they have
    I sob and sob and sob

                                    excited for them
                                    broken in me)

I had the one best friend, who, as she got older, was still alone

        we could talk about our grief
        and
        our pain
        and

                just as I got back from visiting her in Canada

                        she
                        she
                        she rang
             to say that she and he had
                              connected together

                  she rang to say they were engaged
                  and

   again I

   I knew her   grief

   I knew her   excitement
                              and I
                                  I was excited
                              and
                              and yet
                              and yet it
                                      ripped
                                     it rips
                                            to
                                                shreds
                   And I yell out
                "There is no one else
                     in their thirties and forties
                     alone

                except me."
                              it felt
                              it feels
                              it always feels
                              it always will

Poetically Together

feel

and she rings,

she rings, my best friend rings, to say

                                                "I'm pregnant."

And she rings
        the call finishes
    she goes

        And I sitting
                on a park bench

                                    goodbye friend
    And I sitting
            sobbing
                  sobbing before
                                sobbing before
                                                sobbing

                        before

                  God

and asking

                why God why must

                              I

                                  be

  alone

                                                    I

                                                        I
                                    can't take
                                    it anymore

            it's too
                    too too painful

Chapter 16
KATHY—THE LOTTERY AND THE LIE

The bouquet soars! We fight for the false promise!

            All the single girls

            We clutter together, middled before everyone

It soars

            And how I hate it

                                    I am so much the older

                                    It soars false promises

                    Someone catches it

                            and they call it's your turn
                                                    it's your turn

                    marriage now marriage

So falsely
        So so falsely.

                So false.

Chapter 17
GREG–A NEW DIRECTION

Compass flirts with the dice—which way to find a tribe?
Should I edge slowly to the countryside, and in floorboards and coffee shops find a soul symphony sung in duet?
Could northern yellow beaches court and dance the moon and kisses?
Should I fall to the metropolis succession—join the never-ceasing flow to the city's streets, find my tribe within that strangers' tribe?
Where is my tribe?
And I dive back to eHarmony once more.

                ****

        You dance with joy like the sun;
        I walk with you as yellow crowns your head;
        Entwine our fingers, our dreams, our souls!

Chapter 18
KATHY–EHARMONY SCAM

God, let me always be the kindness who delivers your love to others.
I haven't seen him yet, but we write
I haven't held him yet, but we speak.
I haven't felt our lives knit yet, but I am picking up threads to see how they should fit.
Dream wanders into dreams of our life, his hand.
Until...
...until he writes, "I need money to come to you. I need air tickets to touch your hand, to wander our separate paths no longer, to feel them weave closer and closer like heart's surgery."
And I investigate

And friends investigate
And at the end
    at the end
I stand
      alone.
Alone, laboured in vain.
Alone, to wander, not wonder.
Alone on that desolate day.
Yet
yet
there had
there had been words spoken
Words that made me feel so valued, so loved
  There were points of connection, of worlds touching. There were points of conning, of words I wanted to hear. There were puzzles solving and interlocking, and yet…
      no heart
      no truth
      no value

It made me fear, to know the meaning of alone

I remember.

I hoped
I prayed
I breathed into the moments of waiting

                Would there be words I want to hear?
                    Would we be together?
                      Would we know life?

                            I FELT LOVE
                            NO, I *THOUGHT* IT
                            TO BE LOVE

        No
        No

Poetically Together

                    No, it came crashing down
                                when he asked
                                for
                                money
                                to
                                get
                                here—
                                a thousand to
                                get here
                                to
                                have
                                a
                                date

        No.

        No!!
        I knew his words were empty
        I knew his words were what he knew
        each woman
                      each woman
                                  each wanted to hear…

    His captivation was towards my money, and not to me;
    His contacting towards his own soul and theft

I up

I up
      DELETE pressed on the keyboard
I up
  and sorrow slides down me
              puzzled and fooled
  my hope crashing down
              non-connected, just alone

        hope dissociates

loneliness parades
grief holds secrets
grief grasped loneliness and hope crashed.

Who could I trust?
    Are there eyes that are real?
    Are there words that are true?

Chapter 19
KATHY–NO COMPROMISE

You grow up as female with everyone saying, "You're going to get married, going to have children. This is life and how it is promised is how it will be."
And yet
    all memory of past futures (the history of promises made to aunts and older friends and spinsters and the creaking frail-aged lonely limbs) tells them there is no guarantee
    yet you grow up with the earnest past memory, the promise!

"You will get married, you will have children, life is as I say."

and when it doesn't work

    you
        crush
    you
        fold down
                even more

and yet

and yet

    I will not compromise

They urge, "Find somebody anybody!"

I will not compromise

I will not compromise
will not spend my dreams

                      to buy some
                            broken
                                years-long Today

Chapter 20
GREG SURVEYS THE FUTURE

I know, I know, that at the end of all things we shall be entirely free.
I know—and yet the cares mount up and shower my years. And ambitions wind down as age winds up.
And although, although, although there might have come a time when I might have wanted to fly, when I wanted to mount up with wings, when I might have wanted to live as the essence of the potential that is inside me

    might have come

    I stumble

I stumble backwards because I am broken hearted, limited in body, unsure and confused of soul

Chapter 21
KATHY—WHY WON'T EHARMONY DELIVER?

Rain on my face...
I give money away for shelter
I give money to eHarmony month on month
I reach my hand to the keyboard on the cold lonely nights

I tap name and password under the lonely light
There is none...
No shelter, no arms, no breathing beside me, no warmth to pour love and heat into my soul
There is me and this
God, why continue?
Why continue this subscription year on end? Why touch this keyboard seeking a human hand?
Why???
And yet
    somehow a sense
        to

        continue

Chapter 22
GREG–THE RIGHT PRIORITIES

Bite the nail
Stare at the screen
I reach out, amend
eHarmony website, first page, fourth column
Amend the Vital Information to read
    I want to find someone who
    will love God
    more than me
Save, click off, lights out
    Now
        for
            bed.

HEARING

A

NEW

SONG

Greg and Kathy Weller

Chapter 23
KATHY–COUNSELLOR AT YOUTH CAMP

The teenagers stand around.
The teenagers in love with God
They pray, they seek no resistance, they cry, "God, I repent of the stubborn part of me. I am ever only yours.
Take away this stubborn will.
Ever only I am yours. "We receive you in full in truth, at conversion, but we still find our wills too quickly."
They cry, "Break me if necessary"
And even as camp counsellor, I stand
Even after all these years of loving You and trying and falling, and rising to fall again,
Even after change and growth and remedying of childhood damage and the trauma that lurked in quiet and innocent rooms, of knowing grace beyond grace...
I stand, fallible hands
I stand and cry, "God, here I am. Break me"
And He says, He says into my soul, "My beautiful daughter, you have been broken all your life. Go now, be free."
And I leave, fear shed away. I leave the pain of all these years. I leave as your slave, not theirs.
I leave

Chapter 24
KATHY SENDS A WINK TO GREG

He is different
I sit before the keyboard and read
It is night and yet sunlight blushes at the corners of my soul.
He declares on eHarmony that Jesus God comes before spouse
Like me!
Just like me!!
And I nervous reach my hands, fingers like sticks moving, nerves breathless and hoping, stomach like jelly, and send a wink.
A wink, eHarmony's sign of interest, of seeking contact, of seeking a future soul mate
I wink, unexpecting a reply.

I wait, unexpectant

Chapter 25
GREG LOOKS BACK

Till the wink,
Till the wink, I learnt, unrealising, to walk counterfeit, too on-guard to be me. The deep me always hidden, effectively blank.

Under all my vitality, I was blank

In my nonstop rush, I was unnerved and plastic and blank

I lived, the real me unprocessed–for all my life of building big frameworks for nine months courses

I always seemed to be participating whilst migrating from anxiety to anxiety, yet resisting the desire to run.

I was always working for God with all my heart, helping in his name whilst hurting in the captivity of rejection.

I was always waiting in faith that God would help, yet inside always retreating, whenever I needed to interact with more than one person

I was always ministering to others with feelings curled up within.

I was geek by proxy, book reader by default

My brain was sharp, my social senses feared the jungle. Ardour for God packed my day with passion and action, incompetence with men tied my hands. Sounds of love and romance flooded from the cd player, whilst my best years for romance had already gone. No one could defeat me in determination and persistence on a task, but a shadow of the beginning of rejection would be grit in my eyes.

Paper my defence, the structured classroom and mum and the Kings' return my only confident interactions

But maybe that was the past. New possibilities reigned among the broken glass of old sorrows

Adam and Eve beckoned my heart

                                      perhaps we could be new Adam,
                                                    new Eve:

              leaving aside our past,
              to step
              into the future
              with God.

Chapter 26
KATHY–WORDS

He responds!
Wink returns!!
Nervousness walks my room. Does history replay?
There was so recently another, there was so recently another who came as undeserved monster via eHarmony, with promises and lies, who needed $1000 and who sought to crumble and crease my reality for his gain

There were words spoken
So recently that one came, so recently gone...
Now, right now, there is a fresh wink.
The screen blinks, warm.

Is it an old story?

        Is it angel wings?

                Are you heart beat and passion and red joy?

My heart is beating, the excitement grows.

Is this connection truth?

Can this be the one?

                      God only knows
                      Only God

Chapter 27
KATHY'S SONG

Jesus God, I love you and beat your name as a pulse within my heart.
You have taught my heart to sing
You found a dry land for feet that were awash and drowning
You are always my joy and song—long before any man, prime before any man.
You will endure as prime despite my finding—or not—of any man.
You are my path, even if I accompany a husband. You are my joy, while he may hum my heart with joy. I am your companion more deeply than his.
And this one has said it!
While my heart has always declared it to You, I have not found another who would also say it.
Until now
He has declared it to all the world on eHarmony. Black on white, his declaration stands.
And again in our emails!
He has told me, written me, that for each of us, Jesus God must be our first, our prime!
If he knocks at my house door, Jesus first
If he bends his lips to mine, Jesus first
If we travel and dance courtship's path, Jesus first
And even if he bends his knee, ring in hand, it will always ever only be...
... in both our hearts...
Jesus first.
And I know that if we madly passionately love, hold Jesus first, we more truly madly passionately love each other too...
...because we see each other through the love we have for Christ.

Chapter 28
KATHY–GETTING TO KNOW GREG

So many emails, so many texts
I will always be coming to know your soul, am always coming to know your soul, have come to know your soul
I stumble from bed, this new day a blank page. I open your email, and the page fills with words

I open your email and I open your soul
        deepness, non-disposable
I open your deepness

    We promised early, we challenged early
        "Ask me anything"
and day after day after day
each tomorrow
        we come to know
        we share deepness
            each to each other.
We touch souls and it is beautiful.

There is so much here!
We have never met, but in these emails we have met each other deeply
We have never touched, but in these emails
            there is romance and breath
           there is princess and knight
           there is the poised diver waiting
                to leave the highboard
           there is the wanting

We have never kissed, we have never met

There were others I have kissed, but never met deeply
There were others next to me, but never
           the door opening

                              the deepness opening
                              the hearts
                                      known
                                              as hearts

(...sometimes kissing clouds the talking of hearts...)

I love
how
        heart talks to heart
        deep calls to deep
        kaleidoscope to kaleidoscope
        the complex you to the complex me

The physical can wait.
        I am drunk on knowing you
        I am reeled over on the questions that sit between us
        I am imbibed on the answers that parade our souls
I am inebriated on our vulnerability
I am a sot, besotted on being truly honest
We
                We are open pages, loaded and wobbling
                We are unmet physically
                        but so so drunk together
                We are honest and broken
                        each to each
                We are blind drunk and honest
                        plastered and smashed

And by the time we will meet
we will already know
    the deepest beating soul
    the softest honest heart
    the vulnerable broken corners

From day one
    we have poured out our softness

Softness that love
   builds
   as concrete and steel.

Chapter 29
KATHY AND GREG–LONGING TO SERVE GOD TOGETHER

You long to write for God, to talk for God

You have spent your life in your mother's business. You have toiled in your mother's business and have carried her failing wings as she aged and leant forward and died

I see your heart. I see your potential, your hunger to be God's hands. There is mud in you, smeared, but under that are gentle, able hands which can learn God's craft and skills.

How did you know that this morning, I asked Him in prayer if we would be in ministry together. I longed for this and I prayed...

... and within the hour, you, not knowing my prayer, emailed and asked whether I would together work to work God's work together

How could you know? How could you have seen?

There is only One who knew, the One who sees souls and hearts and lives and future and hands

In love, in death, in the unusual shape and the uncut field, let us work together.

Chapter 30
KATHY RECALLS AN OLD PROMISE

And were I to know you'd take so long, so many lonely breaths, so many icy tears, so many black dogs and unseen monsters, so many desperate years, so many lost years–so many decades upon decades...

Thirty slid upon my soul.

Forty boomed upon me as thunder.

I declared in bitterness all those lonely years, that when I met you, that I would hit you for the pain of all those waiting wasting years

Each wasting day loses its meaning, and becomes next day and next day and next year– they roll away like taxi cabs into the night

Greg and Kathy Weller

I knew God had placed this desire for marriage in me
I prayed, "God, unplace this desire from me
                If not of you, unplace
                If not of you, dispose

        And
        My future longings stayed there
        As heavy as
        All the years I had already grieved
        All the years I had kept me pure
        All the cascades of longing multiplied
        All the torrents of waiting magnified
                All the tears
                All the needs

                        And I walk to the shop
                        See couples walk
                        in your hand
                        Jigsaw-complete
                  I know couples kiss
                  With fire, in unity
                  When am I first there?

Grief writes its novel.
Pain writes its poems.

Only the grieved can know them–
Only the lonely and pained truly sing them–
Only their diaries can hold them–
Their battlefields so deep
The maiden's cries unheard by
                      any knight at all
This maiden cries out, "Is there a
                knight even at all?"

And they say, all say, each and every say
"Marry anyone, belief or nil!

Poetically Together

    Come, let me tune your heart–
    I have a new man for you–
              his heart will sing to you."

But as for me, I would rather go through absoluteness of
grief and pain rather than marry someone who
wasn't equal in my heart and frame and beliefs–
else find my psyche hemmed in rising scale, because unevenly yoked,
find grief and pain multiplied, stacked, layered, amplified

        And its hard not listening to everybody
        Because you really want to be with somebody
        But I need that new body
        To be the right some body
        That God has bought into my life.

And
And when we finally
And when we finally met,
I found that grief faded
Faded before hopes fulfilled,
before the knowing that you had
had met all my hopes,
all my deep deep hopes–and
yet so many, very many more.

And I didn't want to smack you–
I wanted to hug you forever.

          And you were a bird with broken wings,
          A bird caught up in one corner of a cage
          A bird so broken

        But I could see the potential in you
        And I could see that all your life
        You had longed to fly for God
                  fly for God

                                    minister for God
And I care
    I long
    I want to
Help you be all God wants you to be
                    To fly
                    To do…

You had sacrificed everything
(even doing ministry)
for your mum

And
And all I wanted
Was to see you do that

And
And
To marry someone unequally yoked–
                how could that be
                when all
                all I wanted
                all I needed
                was to wed a man of God
                and to labour
                together
                forever
                in fervour
                for his name

And how could it happen
How could I walk
With one who didn't walk with God?

All I desire!–
    To serve God with you!

THE

DUET

BEGINS

Greg and Kathy Weller

Chapter 31
THE TWO SING TOGETHER

We strengthen each other. We lean into each other's soul
We dare do that because God allows that
We dare do that because God is the one who brought us here, brought us in rejoicing and freedom and love. As we look, we see all our long hopes for the future sliding into possibility

Let us hold this! Let us not become puzzles for the other to try to understand.

Let us see in each other the heartbeat and soul orchard of a beautiful spirit created and laboured over by an amazing God–and somehow amazingly given to the other to cherish, to nourish, to help fly...

... and to have someone who knows my inner name

Let us be only ever becoming what God would have us be. Let us always be fervently asking him to strip away from us all that is not of Him–He holding our hands, we holding His hand determinedly in each trial, resolving to only live for him in the trial, knowing that nothing will ever happen that is beyond his will nor beyond our strength and our capacity to trust in his will.

And to do this journey with you, my love.
The journey with you!
There's nothing else I can do... or want to do... or will do

Chapter 32
KATHY'S FRIENDS URGE A CHECKING THAT GREG IS ON THE LEVEL

And we say to you, "Reality ripples around you. It must not touch your eyes.

"There was the seeker of the money, there was the farmer and the failure, there was sorrow...

"How is this one to be true?

"He writes you long emails at three am in the morning! How non-local! How half-way-round-the-world-this-scammer-sits-with-evil-intent!

"How non-genuine it feels to all our senses!

"Place your check. Surely asking at least for a photograph is not too much to ask.

"There are so few photos on his eHarmony entries.

"A full-length photo at least!"
"Yes! With a time and date, so we know it's him."

Chapter 33
THE TWO THRILL TOGETHER

Please don't let us become fervently coldhearted. Don't, I beg, let us slide to thrilldead.

No, let us become favoured in our fervour and fever tonight, so sweetly appetited.

Let us be unashamed, hungrily holy and in our souls, touching.

Let us always be driven to God and only His Word. The Bible our undertow that pulls us only ever nearer the Throne.

And to seek Him!!

Not to seek Him from conservatism, nor of fear nor of obligation to family, nor of rebellion, nor of law nor tradition. Let each of us be seeking Him first, the other second.

And our actions—not to be rebellion, not to be tradition, not to be conservatism—simply two lovers rejoicing in God and in each other

And as you call my name even now, you create an instant island where I am alive, alone with you and your singing eyes.

Chapter 34
THE TWO: *"WILL I LOVE YOU MORE THAN MY RIGHT TO BE RIGHT?"*

We are two heart beats away from the events and speeches that shape our world. They would make us under pressure a fox or a dove—they would mentor us and bring us towards tears or conformance.

And so the world proceeds, case by bitter case, incident by self-rights incident, to crash or to drag us through flame.

And if we two were to argue together, would I see just your angry eyes, your hips with hands, your self-righteous soul—or would we love so that our love is despite the other's teary eyes or flaming eyes or furious body stance? Would I love you more than I love my right to be right?

I will never quarantine myself off from you when I am angry, not withhold the sensual mountains, not hide myself from your side. When the deepening threat breathes at our hearts calling to us to make us flee the threat, I will still lean on you. When another comes to entice me, to parade their sideshow and flesh, as want maker and courage taker, as mad butcher of two hearts, to raise lament and desolation and aloneness, we will lean–even at times when there might seem no present reason, we will lean on each other

To love as Christ loved, to care as Christ cared, to give the other liberty as Christ gives–forever gives liberty

He keeps no ledgers of past wrongs done and half atoned for, nor will we. He replays no video of the outplaying of outrageous hurt–nor will we retain them. We choose no database–nor drivers for it. We hand over all resentment to God, if necessary day by day, with weeping–and then the choice of forgetting, of not holding, of not reckoning it significant. Then to put into that place, all our love and devotion to the being you are inside, and the unconditional vibe we had once. Otherwise we strangle ourselves in alternative futures that never have to be. And we also lose, trample underfoot, all ability to market us each one to the other (bitter-sweetly or otherwise)

I'll not be your doctor–but your companion. I'll not be the doctor's receptionist that greets you with reserve–but I will always greet you always with transparency, vulnerability and loving abandon. I'll not be the doctor's notebook–reporting only relevant and sifted facts–but the one who accepts and lives with your right to be self-reforming without fitting into my prescribed mold–you never my alibi, symptom or cure, never my disease not my explanation for the sin that has forever dwelt in my fallen being (although progressively beautifully ameliorated and remediated and remedied by Him).

We are never an institution–we are ever only two beating hearts, seeking the other's breath. We will not seek to rule each other by dividing the other into weaknesses and conquering them by conquering their weaknesses first. We will not see each other as a combination of sub systems but always as the full person they are and have been in the past and will be in the future. We will not see the other as something for the recycle bin, either they as our partner or any component of their soul. You are not a version number on the way to our better place or my better place or your better place

I will let you get under my skin, behind my defences, between my heart beats.

Forever through life–our joint living and our joint dying.

Chapter 35
KATHY HEARS HER FRIENDS

To my friends, I say I will.
You are concerned.
    And though I am here, in his thoughts and prayers,
    And though I have a bounty, to not fritter away
    I hear your love
             I know your caution and concern
    I have lived all my years your acceptance of all my tears.
    When the world had broken me, you had held me.
    When I was bloodied, your tears washed my wounds
    When I was stubborn and blind, your hands opened my eyes.
    You have handed me back my years
             (all these many many tears
            and black days, blacker nights).
    There is life, which stops–and there is you.
    So yes, I will ask for his pastor's contact
    And talk to him about this man.
    So yes, I will ask for photos
    Current and showing all his height.
    To you who fled the water from my eyes
    These many many times,
    To you who have shone in my heart
    All our maiden smiles
    For us who are frail and strong
            sisters and sharing
            joy and love and
            support and succour
    I will hear you
        I hear your heart.

Chapter 36
GREG RECEIVES THE REQUEST WHILST WALKING

I push up the hill, walking.

Bright sun touches, warms the chill day.

On a day like this, physical bounds are meek, pliant, just steps to a healthier, recovering me, the physio at journey's end a guide from a tangled past to a new coming future.

I had always bad posture, I leant forward habitually. Mum had died because of a stoop slid too far, and I was determined it wasn't going to happen to me

By God's grace–*always* by God's grace.

I had done the exercises–ruthlessly. Basketball lay-ups and workouts (just me and myself there) had been excellent.

I pounded the street headlong, endorphins finding melody.

A text came in–from she, the one had taken reality and reclothed it in new yellows and vibrance and heat, from the one that had reached out and re-animated deeply everything, all the corners of my life.

My dear

My friends have asked, my old and closest friends, for me to get your pastor's number. To chat to him. To find out a little more about you.

And here I send a photo of me, taken just the other day. Can you send a photo of you, so we can see each other more truly.

I know its unnecessary, but my dearest friends, my oldest, have seen it wise.

In love you are my heart.

Amid athlete's-high on this rising hill, I thought, why not.

Still, a little concern poured into the thought. I wasn't fitting in with the new church folk. They were strangers and so few left of the old familiar ones. They were older, had established connections–tight knit, and sitting in closed groups, it seemed to me. Only three or four had had friendly chats–and I single, they married–older and younger–so that distance reigned in our every talk.

And rejection, from when I was 15, mixed and hung heavily in every interaction.

Still, I texted back the pastor's name and phone, with a prayer "God's will be done (now and always and forever)".

Endorphins thrilled the hill. I strode out. The hernia had healed, my heart danced the fast walk's high. It's time to run, put my life together, lose my aloneness with this beautiful one, dance as Adam and Eve, start our beginning.

Phone music pumped vigour. This kid is doing OK, Life is doing OK. I can laugh at past misunderstandings, mock at minutiae. I can leave behind every hurt, every fall.

How rightness and sun flood into the warming, cloudless day! I rise up to my music and the endorphin power play

The stiller air in the valley sang as I neared the physio's rooms.

****

> Were our hearts banded together
> Were marriage so bedded down
> Our hearts would still sing forever
> Our joy always our forever crown.

Chapter 37
GREG LEAVES THE PHYSIO, TIRED

The bus jostled the streets, I rumbled homewards in the near dark.
Physio session had done well. I was tired.
Weariness questioned my eyes. Fog circled, found room in my brain.
Still, there was something yet to do—somehow.
Kathy had requested photos of me.
Quirky would be good, I thought.
Off the bus—dare the long hill home.
Tired, triumphant, but duty comes soon...
In the house.
Prep the dinner!

> You are melody partner
> You give my soul flight
> I have found wings
> I flutter, dive with delight

Chapter 38
GREG AND THE QUIRKY PHOTO

It's late and I'm tired.

Still, the promise remains.

It isn't necessary, fatigue stammered at me, to do a good job, just a quick job–get photos done, photos gone. (Oh, KATHY, please forgive me, please give me acceptance for my two left feet.)

Shorts on. Long socks on.

Two jumpers in the chill. (I resisted all the foolishness of a two year old, slammed shut the door on foolishness and let it in through all the windows).

I knew I'd look good with some comic idiot poses with the oversize acoustic guitar.

                  As doped as Adam was–
                  no sense of perspective as
                  he let Eve eat the apple.

So thrilled as Adam
So wrong as Judas
Falling into heartbeats of foolishness
And sorrow, by inaction, becomes so so found.

Some throw-away lines printed large as A4 on the laser printer.

Yup, quirky, goofball, personality plus.

No need for cool. Let ego disappear and humble realness be the light.

Pose and

SNAP

pose and new sign and

                  SNAP

                      guitar high in the air and new
                            sign
                            SNAP

New one

            SNAP

                        SNAP

Yup

Light and dark and colours splayed on paper

Done

Sent

                                              Bed!

Chapter 39
KATHY VIEWS THE PHOTOS

This picture!
He touches a different time, walking over white socks rising impossibly high.
I know his soul, yes.

But there were my dreams. I dreamt my man would look such, and his face as such, his mannerisms to mix this daydream with that movie set in the gentle hours of a summer dream.

And I say: be gentle to your friend and distant to your imagination. False expectations and false pictures of what your heart's breath of a man should look like tumble you to rodeo, stumble you too far from neutral, judo you too too near to chains to see what you have before you.

Dreams that are solid are simply chains. They hold no proof, they spurn reality and accountability.

He suddenly stands too foreign–or too old–by mistake and by hopes that dash.

And to you, my one I know by heart, I stumble because at this moment you are too too alien from my heart's presented dream.

Chapter 40
KATHY WRITES

I email you this morning, my love, to say I need time.

Thank you for the photos. I know there is a song of hope interleaving into our lives, into our hands. But taking time is wise, as is caution.

We hold grace and prayer and walking with God. He holds our times, and how times unfold

I need some time.

Chapter 41
GREG STANDS IN PERIL

    Denial pushes back at reluctant introspection. It seems a logical deduction that I live in a dangerous moment.
    She is.... I could lose her.
    My emotions move like unknown strangers I can't reach
    They bounce on the border of rejection fears. You, Kathy, took away loneliness. I had sadder and happier eyes. I had hope—a lightning dance.

                              God was building a still unknown me.
                              It probably wouldn't have lasted.

                              I have grown up with rejection.
                              I see myself as infant before others' eyes
                              So alone

I am in a soul I have never known

Call to God for aid.
                              I stand lonelier than a hermit.

I've loved and lost

              as expected.

                      You take away everyone, O God.
                      Yet I will still trust you.

Chapter 42
KATHY RE-EVALUATES HER JUDGMENT OF THE PHOTOS

All my life, I have waited. All my life, I have sought a one.

I hoped there would come a one who would see the inside me. To see the breathing me under the outer. To not judge.

And yet I have taken the place of the judgers. I have been convicted of wrong–I have been the judge, immediately, of your outside! I have lessened you in my sight because of externals.

I was wrong and begin again, my friend.

Let us each hug the other unseen one in truth. And in return each of us dares to be the unseen inside in our action.

So each of us sheds the illusion and the mask and the false and the shutters. We choose to stand beating heart to beating heart, soul in hand to soul in hand, transparent hopes and rips and tears to transparent hopes and rips and tears

Real to real

Breath to breath

Human to human

Humans breathing reality into each other's soul

Chapter 43
GREG'S INTERNET AND EHARMONY ARE DOWN

I have tried.

The internet lights move in vain, wishing but not forming reality.

I have tried.

Tried to write her the daily email

The internet hunkers into stillness, slides into sleep

Reboot, restart, test cables.

Type the same words. Recreate the same mouse movements.

                                                      Find the same result.

The internet offers no useful thing–as the hours tick on.

Poetically Together

A prayer for just a *momentary* internet recovery
A prayer for just one email to her, and for one email back.
A prayer, knowing a history of how God answers.
Then a quick typing: "The internet is not working. Can I have your phone number? Then I can ring you... or we can wait till tomorrow..."
Sent
For the first time that night, a success! *Sent!*
I wait with sweat and stilled fingers. Waiting. Praying......
somehow, an email back
...a number!
I praise God and reach toward the phone.

****

May our love flow always
As life-giving joy.

Chapter 44
THE TWO MAKE THEIR FIRST PHONE CALL

I dialled her number, watching the trembling I felt in hands and stomach.
    I waited. I checked the number.
    "Hello?"
    "Uh, hello! How are you?"
    And the voice was not what either of us had expected. We had made up a voice inside our heads, heard it whenever we sat to read an email...
    But Kathy's beautiful rich Australian twang, Greg's chirpy chipmunk of a voice, had no relation to what we had heard consistently, constantly, richly in our heads...
    We rolled smoothly on, chatting and laughing and talking about things only we would know.
    Minutes slid to two hours of beauty.
    We said goodbye.
    Each of us hung up, and stared at the phone, replayed in our heads the stranger's voice which had said all the things only we could know.
    Secrets and yet strangers.

We had learned each other from the inside out. Weeks of Greg daring Kathy to ask him anything, the asking of heavy questions, the joy of continuing deep conversations for each of us–we had learnt and had come to know each other deeply.

In the photos and in the phone, we encounter the tent, the body, in which the other lives.

New tent, same deep deep soul.

****

> May I always sing you
> A symphony, never ending, living
> A future deep and hoping, embracing
> A new normal ever-changing
> Ever-changing: our soul under His hand.
>
> That you love me folds down into my soul
> a thousand roses, ten thousand guitar
> notes, a million scattering doves.
>
> And oh, to have your warm cheek
> touching mine.

Near you, the dawn
Would kiss the beaches' waves.
I long to kiss beauty,
to know and kiss your lips.

Chapter 45
THE TWO RESOLVE TO ALWAYS FREELY ALLOW THEMSELVES TO SELF-EVALUATE AND SELF-CHANGE

I'll not play games with you: that day by day, year by year, my weaving and hiding build a blog that never can be unwritten–till I am alienated from you, two strangers in one flesh, two that know neither war nor peace.

Nor to run from you, nor avoid you, because that does the above, by default.

No, I'll not sin against you.

Instead, let our souls kneel transparently, always by choice, each morning, as we pray, each for the other. We know we miss God's heart, the compassionate yearning of God and His Kingdom, when we walk with human hearts asking less than each other yearns to give, when we walk into pastures less green than He longs to give.

We have no right to give Him advice. We two are only dead ones whom he has made alive. We two are only lies and legends now being made flesh. We two are children training and children dearly loved. We two are sometimes (never the "always" (so human, so human)) in unity with Christ and long, long to be as often in unity with each other.

Let us each become diverted love, diverting from all when the other's heart cries. Let us become mirror love, that in our actions and order, the world sees Christ's love

Let us two run for The First Two Human's prize (Adam and Eve), step by step, sheaf by sheaf, turn by turn, whirlwind by whirlwind. We run as whirlwind, knowing He steers even the whirlwind.

May we never give Him up. May us, each one, never give the other up. May we never leave the other as God never leaves us each one, in service, in respect, in courage, and in compassion...

...and in love, above all!!

Above all, in love!!

In love that avoids complication, that hates deception. In love never fading away from the growing, changing heart. Love that persists despite obstacles, love that remains despite turmoil, love that takes the long road when it's right.

Let us two grow towards God with all our heart. As we, each one, unafraid, change and flourish, God is well able to change each of us so we are still one in unity–all he asks is that we hug love for him, obey his Bible commandments always with all our hearts, obey in sun and in fire, knowing He is well able to change each of us each one, to keep us in harmony.

May we stumble together towards marriage, stumble our delighted dance, stumble and dance and off-key sing, before a God who yearns for each of us more than each yearns for the other

Chapter 46
GREG PREPARES FOR HIS DRIVING TEST

I arise
Butterflies caress fear
Today the driving test.
Today the gateway to driving down to visit.
Today I will have the same dream in newer substance.
Today your calling softness will find a abler strategy
Today the test, today the success of inheritance-money spent on twenty lessons.
Today
Today the tiredness of last night presses at the creases around the eyes. Sleep had alertly kept distance. Tired, but I ring her and together briefly pray for His extravagant kindness.

On to the long wait till the test!

****

You O God
Held your cross
Held your pleading for me

Held till 'twas done.

Chapter 47
GREG AND THE DRIVING TEST

The driving examiner approaching, my driving instructor smiling, chatting, fading to her car.
I sit there, and at his bidding, exhibit brake lights, headlights, the on and the off.
Official clipboard holds down the paper which will hold the mark
And we off
Past the school–carefully I drive at 40
Onto the main road. Change lane at speed. Slow at the sign. Slow to stop (mind the pedestrian.)

Me talking through the blizzard of nerves and fatigue, my voice spilling into the quiet car:- "approaching lights... release accelerator... touch brake briefly... blinker on... left lane, left lane.... blinker off... brake... brake... brake..."

The examiner smiling.

"Check .... all clear!...

"Lights change... brake release and slide... accelerator now... across slowly slowly... accelerate.... now..."

On and on, each step verbalised to push back nerves and tiredness and competing thoughts.

The examiner's smiles tickled to broadness

On to the long long road past two schools.

The examiner said the words, "Down the street and back into the Testing Office."

Almost finished. Almost the licence.

Almost the weariness had overwhelmed

And so close, so close

Weariness slow-talked my brain to torpor

First school done. So close, let's get this done.

Speed up

Speed up

Speed up

"You had better slow down. You're almost ten K over the limit."

I looked down at the speedo

50...

in a 40 zone. I had failed.

> The future unlimited when we were young.
> The future so limited now when one has failed.

Chapter 48
GREG RINGS KATHY AND TELLS HER OF CHANGED PLANS

My eyes had dreams, but now I remain unchanged
I have failed. There is no bigger sky.
I failed, and I have failed you, my love.

I can't come Saturday as we had planned. I had wanted to be with you just a few hours, just to feel the edges of love underline the day's movements, to feel gold tint and paints colour in the moments we spend together. To hold you, however briefly.

....then to scurry home.

To visit and fade quickly so you could evaluate your feelings (for I believe a woman knows within 30 seconds of meeting face to face whether their future is placed within shared or separate cups.)

I would have seen you for two hours, then left

We would wend our way home, plotting when and how we would--or would not-- meet again.

But you are not here, nor will be.

I am not with you, nor can be for a while.

And she? "I might have an idea. Leave it with me, leave it with me..."

And we onto other things, finding again the deeper conversation.

****

    Oh, that fever might melt in our hands
    That I might kiss you while gazing on your heart.

Chapter 49
GREG READS THE EMAIL ABOUT KATHY COMING TO HIS TOWN

She will come
She and a friend will come
They will come to my town
They will sit and we will have lunch together
And I up
And I up and find the restaurant–there was only one that it could possibly be. I up and there for lunch to role play the scenario, sitting, choosing, planning, sampling.
Then home to confirm and shave.

****

    Tonight, the waiting stands
    too long between us,
    my love!

Chapter 50
AT THE RESTAURANT

Walking long the street
Is it him? Is it him?
    (So nervous, so nervous)

Stand near the restaurant, scanning
Is it her? Is it her?
    (Face switched to "amiable" permanently, in case)

I see him! He is real!
I had so so wondered...
    (A sigh of relief, a long breath in.)

She is taller than I thought
Her hair dances red, embraces the sun

(The time has come, the traveller has come.)

He looks worried
But it must be him
    (Should we kiss? Should we smile with restraint?)

"Hi, so great to finally meet!"
    (Tension flattens all feelings.
    Still, somewhere, happiness smiles.)

"This is my friend."
    (My trusted friend, my dearest sensible friend.)

"Good to meet you" (to her friend)
    (I had so preferred she weren't here)

    "Shall we go in?"
And we file into the cafe, so crowded so crowded
Shuffle and slide and apologise our way to a table in the centre
"This is for you, my love."
A present, a first present
(And inwardly, a dance of joy.)
Push out the chair into the limited gap, half bend our way into sitting.
"How was the trip?"
    (So close - less than 30 cm between our two chairs)
"I stayed with my friend last night, so it was an easy trip.
she often comes to Toowoomba."
    (Connection established, going well.)

"Oh, so good."
    (I chuckle at the hours I had spent yesterday writing detailed instructions about how to find the restaurant—I had left nothing out.
    In fact, there was actually nothing that had needed to be said.)

"Greg," the friend says. "I have a question."
"Sure"

"A friend I had was asking if I could ask you–she is in her forties and was wondering for herself... Are there Christian virgin men over 40?"

And I, longing to be confident and cool before Kathy, happily expressed my opinion. Talked in the crowded restaurant while the food came and went. Talked whilst Kathy shrank, her song lost, longing for the ground to swallow her whilst breathing. Her old old friend had done such a thing as might drive this man's interest to bemusement and loss.

And back and forward, and back and forward...

(And Greg's sister ringing to give him an out–somehow, he continuing on.)

And was the whole café listening to my embarrassment, as the topic dragged on.

At last, like some acne spot, the moment went away. Conversation turned to safer things.

And shortly, my friend excused herself and we were alone!
But all too done too soon
A brief brief walk and suddenly the afternoon slipped away
And she was gone.
Gone with her friend.

****

I make a pledge of flesh, my heart.
It dances for you inside its glad tent of joy

Chapter 51
GREG REFLECTS

She texted as they were driving
We poured love into the moments
She was gone too quickly
And in weeks, long weeks, another driving test
Maybe then, maybe then, I will visit her.

****

Passion and serenade
Fever and fervour
You are so far, yet so close.

Chapter 52
GREG MAKES HIS PLANS

I have prepared
There is a motel room, and nearby there is her and her beautiful home.
This weekend I bus down to be with her.

****

> So tired of one heartbeat
> Mourning an empty hand.
> I offer my heart to God
> I offer my heart to you.

Chapter 53
THE TWO–AFTER <u>THAT</u> WEEKEND

I held a possibility that held my world. Freedom had come. After decades of tying myself up, of being tied, I had become free.

At the camp, praying all my heart, praying all my yearning, seeking to give away my insecurity and depression to God, I prayed, "God, break me."

And I had felt his answer come. "You've been broken all your life. Now you are free."

And I was free to be me before people, free to step away from depression, free to leave fakeness behind, free to care and love without hesitation.

And three days later, I had seen you, I had shown an interest, I had sent you an eHarmony wink, you had responded. We had begun the dance–I, we had both come a step forward despite our fear, through the brooding fear to see what God had in store for us

And it was good

Now the black dog has galloped me to darkness. I have lost you (or my hope of you), I have lost the new me I was getting to know.

It might not have gone well. Last night at mini golf she was always two holes ahead of me, and when i finally caught up, she was a brief sentence then she skipped forward again.

Mono syllables on the way home.

I had tried all my best jokes

I had ignored the nerves, letting the adrenaline lift me to the better story, the better joke

All my witticisms like machine guns seeking to find her smile

All of a sudden it is black–I can't see me, can't see the world. There is only the sound of blackness and the breathing of my anguish. It comes into me. I am shuttered down and fear rages inside this room. I am trapped in the hollow terrible aloneness in the hollow me. This feeling that would crush me drives me to my own destruction.

From suddenly everything to suddenly nothing–not even me

He had come down for our first weekend. He had come off the bus, saying embarrassment at his clothes and had asked me to take him to Kmart for new clothes. He quickly found a top and bustled into the dressing room to try it on–and remained in there twenty minutes. Twenty minutes!!–then came out and asked me to get the next size down in the same t-shirt!!!

My brain was dancing dreams of rage.

And alone in the paper-thin walls of the hotel booked online–at an excellent price–I tried to sleep whilst the person four rooms away ratcheted their throat to ever-increasing achievement.

It didn't go ok and I can't sleep.

Somewhere there is a muted waterfall of destruction

And we on the road–me showing this man the sights of the Gold Coast. And he talked a little, then more. It ran like rivers over the car, into my ears, sopping and sogging into my mind and soul. Too much, too much! (You flood my head!)

But I fought, I tried–but his unending mouth led me captive, and this unquiet one drives acceptance to incapability.

(If a dice rolled a hundred times, it could never show two. Never a two!)

And the next morning, nerves and tension tangled with my stomach and head and I texted:

"I can't see you today"

And I understand he went home on the bus.

Skipping out of my life, my hopes, my possibilities

And in now skips and sledgehammers this enraged monster that stalks me. This black dog that tears me.

And in the morning, the text, "I can't see you today."

It is somehow expected

Stagger up, shower, home on the bus.

Everything is fine. Sitting slowly, the bus jerking quickly.

While I am slouching into comfort, there's two noisily entering the bus

They sit just across the aisle from me. She pregnant–and he chattering, rattling like unending raindrops on roofs.

Chattering me to exhaustion

I realise it's going to be a long trip.

I sigh.

And I ring, I ring my friend and sob out my blackness and blindness. There had been something there

I remember the restaurant, my girl friend there for safety. The talk and feel so full of possibility

I remember the long phone talks and chats between us–two hours talking flying by as if nothing

I remember the shared times of prayer on the phone. Sensing his love for God, his commitment

Now I submitting inside to the monster that prowls.

"I can't take it. I will die. I will take my life"

And my best friend urgently calling to me

On the phone, she chats urgently to me, to the me buried and mauled by the serrated teethed monster. Calling, "I will come. I will come. I will catch the plane tonight. Let me...

While I slouch into comfort, there's two noisily entering the bus

They sit just across the aisle from me. She pregnant–and he chattering, rattling like unending raindrops on roofs.

Chattering me to exhaustion

I realise it's going to be a long trip.

I sigh.

What is wrong that he won't be quiet, this man on the bus?

I teeter teaspoons on a pin in my head and see how long before he starts again. He starts and shatters my concentration

The teaspoon mentally clatters

And...

Yes, he's off again

And again

And again

Exit at Helensvale station, happy to be away from the yammer and the sledge pounding and pounding in my brain

I wonder (only briefly) if I was ever like that.

Could!

Was!
Were!!
"Oh God, isn't that true?" I breathe to the Eternal One who always hears.

On the phone, she chats urgently to me, to the me buried and mauled by the serrated teethed monster. Calling, "I will come. I will come. I will catch the plane tonight. Let me...

...help."

Help, who can help? Who comes near this hell that rips to shreds, that devours from the inside out?

Who??
But she cares
There is one who cares
There is some light within the darkness.
And I find some small door to exit–at least for now–the despair-caged me.
I am a skinless man; I bleed everywhere.
How did you leave, why did you leave?
I don't deserve you, I am of no worth; but I want to scream that I lost you.
I know no beauty, I roll side to side.
I sink down into the bed.
Down to non-responsive. Down to obscurity. Down to nothing. Down to unfindable.

I am skinless. I feel that I should feel nothing, that it was to be expected, that all who know me reject me.

There is blood inside; there is blood loss from my hands; there is blood where I have walked

And it's somehow what I expected.
The world glitters through the bedroom curtain, and I run inside me.
I am unknown and choose to be unknown. I am loss and will be lost

I thud me. It is no consequence, I am ugliness and I paint my world with enduring ugly.

There is blood inside; there is blood loss from my hands; there is blood where I have walked

It's somehow what I expected.

Rejection lies so deep inside me, I have learnt my lesson so clearly that it has shaped my sky, it has shaped my breath. I force myself into service and titles of service and institutions of service–because then I am forever pouring me out like cool calming living water and it avoids me being rejected, because I am always rejecting me first

She did as I would also have done.

We were Eve and Adam discovering. We were Juliet and Romeo defying all the marriage norms of mediocrity. We were gentle love overcoming the world of hate and gratification.

We were

We were big

But...

...it was too big

I had prayed all my life for a man like this. Now he is too here and too real

Sometimes there are streets and avenues and one way directions–but this is crossroads.

What am I doing? Haven't I waited for a man like this all my life? Haven't I wanted to be loved? Haven't I wanted to be held? Haven't I wanted someone to see past the outside and see the within? Isn't this what this person is, what this person does?

She is of sound mind and judgement. She saw through my weakness and nervousness and uncertainty to know what I was

I Am Reject

The world is as it should be.

And I run into protective mode. It's easier to cut myself off from all feeling, from hope, from others.

I

am

alone

cut off

there is no land of the living that would want me

I do not want me...

...but I choose not to die.

I will fight. I am still the squashed rejected autopilot me but I will survive.

I will will the blood on the skinless me to stay on it's appointed path, as I stay also my mind, in service.

Let me learn Greek, the most exact language ever, that I am surrounded by exactitude. And in exactness, my skinless blood will stay its exact course

She was wise–

she saw

she chose wisely

Let me choose my next step in the world of normal

The so difficult words from my counsellor on the phone: "You have wanted this all your life ... here is the person you wanted. Are you running scared? You will lose what you wanted. You have to choose what you want to do..."

This is the third day since he went. I drown, I break air to gulp and gasp. Is it too late?
Too late for the moment
Too late for the kissing, too late for the laughing and looking and catching the eye in a lingering flame
Before God
Before God, what have I done
If
If I lose
If I lose a man from God, a man supplied by God
An aha moment, the pulling away of blindness
As if
As if God...
There is symmetry in tightness, in cyclonic force held in fists.
There is ended the beginning, there is ended the ending
There is there and I am here.
But there is chaos and rejection and lost hope and anger that push as newcomers into a small village that does not want them.

                   I bid them go
                   but they stay

I breathe
In the heat of my car, I breathe. I am caught in emotion and I would rather not be here
In the racing pulse and heart, I would not be here.
I touch the Greek book.
       It is all I know.
She, she had taught me to love, had taught me feeling, had taught me nakedness of soul.
    My soul is ugly.
        I tuck it inside me
           I had hoped she could teach

           Teach me realness

                    I touch the Greek book
                    I understand this
This rigour, this tightness
I
I

       I do not understand me.

Pack me away.
Pack me inside, grip and fist.
As if…
As if God said to me, "You've prayed to me for over 30 years for a man of God and I have just given you that gift. Now you want to throw that gift away? Do you want to just run away and not have what you've asked for, what you've prayed for all your life?"
Slapped
I'm about to lose something that I've wanted all my life
I don't want to be alone
Alone forever
Reach out, reach out or lose this
Reach out as friends
Reach out and rebuild
Reach out as friend
Reach out and start as friends
Reach out, realising this has not been about him: it was about me. It was about my fears; it was about the reality. It was that he was the real thing
Stop running
Warily I eye this soul in my fist
              Suddenly I run
                     I up
                     I out the door
                     New open licence in my hand, I in the car
                     Drive slowly, carefully…
                     …but drive
                     My soul chatters and caterwauls
                     It is a soul I don't understand
                     I chase rigour in how I move the car,
                            with preciseness in turn,

in accuracy and precision of blinker.
I drive to commit retail!
Stop
Stop running
Stop hesitating
Choose to reach out and make this happen because Greg was the one God had for me
And...
...and I will learn patience...
... so that 20 minutes in the dressing room
is not too long
I will place myself in situations of patience, to drive behind slow
drivers. Do 40 km/hr and learn.
I will learn slowness in awaiting an outcome

There is at least one graceful moment passed. In the crisis I had ended it gently. I could have sought to manipulate and shape him and wrestle him to my perceived sovereign decree and edict and shape–but then I would be changing the him that God has made him to be.

And *that* is not my job. That is *never* my job. It will *not* be my job–or my romance.

Her SMS sat on his phone.

He had started his Greek journey, had poured bargains into his shopping bag, and was sitting in his car in the late afternoon dancing sun, and his licence, new and achieved and permanent, lay on the passenger seat beside him.

Her SMS sat on his phone, an unknown, an uncertainty touching hope. He committed himself to seeking her best, and opened the SMS.

Her words spilled into the car

"*Hello friend*

"*Both of us were lonely and tried to fit six months into three weeks. Crazy really, hey?*

"*I truly believe for a relationship to have a firm foundation, a deep friendship needs to be built. And I thought we'd do that in marriage, but while you were here, I realise we don't know each other at all. The most beautiful thing we have in common is a mighty God which is a great foundation. But what else do we have in common? Time hasn't been taken to just get to know each other...*

"*How are you travelling in yourself, friend? I'm excited to get to know you more, building a friendship, holding each other in prayer.*

"*I love God conversations with you. May we grow together in God in our contact.*

"*Be blessed today. I covered you in prayer on my walk this morning.*

"Deep blessings to you.
"Kathy"
And he: "Yes, Yes.
"Yes, dear heart.
"Because I choose, because God chose, because I love and you love."

Chapter 54
GREG ARRANGES HIS FIRST CAR TRIP TO THE COAST

I have already driven halfway to her city and back, then taken the last motorway turnoff before tolls...

...I had got lost

I had pulled into a service station, realised I couldn't work out how to use the petrol pump, asked instructions from the service station operator. He, slightly disbelieving, showed me...

I had to return to the operator to pay, slightly embarrassed.

The bill paid, I got back in the car, then realised I didn't know the way home... I again walked up to the operator's counter, this time to ask him the way to my town. He had just sighed, then reached under the counter, pulled the top sheet off a centimetre high pile of photocopied directions to Toowoomba, passed it to me, and went back to work without pausing. Apparently, I had not been the first to ask!

I had arrived home eventually....

But tonight, tonight I had talked to her. I had pondered and then had decided... I told her I would catch the *bus* down like before–after all, I had only so recently got my licence.

But an idea had grown.

While I slept, the idea had sat silent in its growing till 3 am, then it had decided itself awake. I would drive the car down there at 4am (just one hour away), drive to her place, and park just out of sight. Then I would ring her and ask if she could come and get me. She would assume the bus had arrived, and bustle out to the car to start the engine!

And I would be...

I would be leaning against the wall and nonchalantly say, "Hey, before you go out somewhere, could we have a cuppa and catch up?"

Done!

I slid out of bed.

Poetically Together

****

> She spreads fragrance over my soul
> This sweet sweet morn.

Chapter 55
GREG AND THE EARLY MORNING WAIT

Easing into the car park at 6:30am.
Nind Street sprawled beside me, untouched in the early morning
Only one hour and I would surprise her
Only one hour
The phone rang.
Unbelieving, I read and re-read the information. It was her.
I couldn't not answer–after all, that would cause alarm.
So I cleared my throat and lifted the receiver.
"Hi," I said.
"Hi!" came her voice. "Whereabouts are you?"
I blinked.
"Pardon?"
"I was wondering where you were. I thought you'd ring just before you got on the bus."
"Um." Thoughts raced furiously. I couldn't lie–was there any way I could avoid the question?
No…
Nothing! I had nothing at all!
"Where are you?"
"Umm, I'm in Nind Street."
"*Nind* Street? What are you doing there?"
And so the story had to be told her.
We laughed
and I had not lied.

****

> Let poets kiss our dreams,
> Let thorns never clog our souls.

Chapter 56
GREG REJOICES

Blow the horn, stamp out the past. I have found the one.
If war comes, I am your knight.
When the nub comes, I'll take the rub.
When the leap comes, I'll risk the plunge

In you, I return to my humanity.
In you, I leave my ice and snow.
By you a heart beats again.
For you, my heart and beyond-friend

Your grace as ornament on you.
Your chaos and daring so sweet.
Your cheek and teasing and caring...

Chapter 57
KATHY REJOICES

We dance in courtship
He comes with flowers and exchanges them for my heart
He touches my hand and cheek, and goose bumps play my nerves and skin
He drives me away to beach and sunsets and heaven on earth
Every breeze brushing my cheek has new meaning
   Three days a week he comes to my home town and stays two streets away. And three mornings a week he is early at my porch–and returns in love the heart he stole away as he left the night before.

Chapter 58
THE TWO ON THE NIGHT SANDS

September dances. Our second month kisses our hearts like fireflies.
You and I kiss–like fugitives we kiss (we are but names to each the other's family; there is all too little time. I gulp all of your heart; there is no time for others.)
Our families lie behind our attention like unknown libraries.
You have lit my flame heart, my breathing bathes in smiles, you attract impossibly more than gravity. You pour water and transparency, and in us sincerity grows its flower. We dance so close–with too few hours for others.

There is only us and flame.

"There is a Sand Sculpture festival. Would you like to go?"
And Greg up and secret preparations, the purchases, the cutting, the parking…
The warm air caresses us as I would to you,
                        I hug anticipation,
                                   I would be near your shore
                    and look, the shore!
"This one looks like a wrecked, rotted ship
              "and this one–how the colours and vibrance?"
                    "The sand, it's only sand, but it forms boxes and people
                            and frames near people"

and the modulating, tantalizing splashing on the shore

                this swimming shore
                this warm shore
                this hand-in-hand shore

                this shore of breathing and nearness
    and
    and
we stand on the balcony above the sculptures, and
                            "I have some food–are you hungry?"

Greg and Kathy Weller

                  "Sounds so good."
                  "Do you want to go down and feast,
                        picnic on the beach?"

and she:
                  "Are you sure?"

                  "Absolutely, I have a backpack
                  full of food."

                  "Umm" and a pause

and inside, disruption pushes in, rolls delight to doubt, rugs the fire to smoulder.
    Muggers and others have attacked
    on dark beaches, and
I look around . . . shadows have come from their slumbers and walk the long long beach,
they parade their insolence. The sun as policeman has abandoned this place. But he...

                        I look and know him
        I look and trust him
              but
              but how
              but how could he know
              know of muggings
              and scattered sharps
              and those sleeping in bushes
              and the murders
              and

      But I know him. And
for him, I: "Just a little way down,
        perhaps here in the light?"
    A prayer
    A deep prayer

            And we down
                        down into this brooding land

Poetically Together

              down, praying it leaves us alone.

And Greg spreads the picnic
    smooths the hard hard sand
    where too insolent it rises
    and she sits
    and he smiles
        and
        out comes cheese upon cheese upon cheese
        a platter, each cheese plated
            touched with spice
            or nut
            or the sweetness

        and placed in love there
            ham
            and
            salami
            and
            sliced beef
            and
            water
(how my love loves water)
            and cups
            and filling
            and looking

            and she is here
            and I am here
                  (us two, us survivors)

    and

"Is someone else coming?" and a teasing smile
"No. \<a laugh\> Why?"
"There is so much here. You have built us a feast. Thank you."
And we laugh and eat
And before us parades the

                walkers, the seers
                the security guards on beach buggies
                the conservative father and the scattering children,
                the mother, and the teenager hearing another's call

    and we eat and drink
    eat in safety
    eat near the pirates and ship
                    and the scattered ship-wrecked boxes
                        scattered, just sand over sand and in sand

                        holding their shape
                        this beautiful night

and drifting across the hard sand
        voices
        voices of
    "coming of age" teens

                    dancing her new joy
                    and he his new new voice
                walking
                "Hey,

                Hey, look at that one over there
                The couple of low set figures"

                    "Let's look"
                            "Let's"
                            and Greg calls out quickly,
                            "We're not sand sculptures"
                    and "uh"
                "uh sorry"
        and the walking away
                a little in haste

    and we eat and drink
        eat in safety

Poetically Together

      eat near the emptying plates
           (though still
                    still so full)

and the packing
and the rising
and the
        dune becomes as if never touched

   and Greg lifts up the weight
                    up to shoulders
  and

we "let's look at the sculptures"
and
we stroll
and
greet the security guard
and others
(how Kathy does the greeting and chatting
                so friendly
                so as Christ
                so with love
                so in God)

   And we up
       we up the stairs
       we up to return to the pavement

and
       the beautiful two
                          crazy and unfettered and
     loving and living
         though with sickness

     we see the two

"Debra and Wayne," Kathy says.
   "Look, its Debra and Wayne."

And he: "Who?"

"My cousins, my beautiful cousins."

And we emerge as pirates from the shore
   and greet the first two
         the first two relatives
         the first two dear dear friends
         of she, my new dear friend:

And "hi"
and "hi"
   and introductions
   and laughing
   and crystalling a little the new new moon-kissed memory

         The family begins to meet!

Chapter 59
MELODY MAKER

It is said that God allows two lovers to sing
Then He comes alongside to provide the harmony
But what is even more true is that He is also the One who teaches each one to sing their own melody more truly every day.
So then God combines the voices together both in melody and in his harmony, deeper and richer and purer and truer to who they really are.

Chapter 60
GREG IS AMAZED

How have you woken me up?
How do I look around and see the field that once was my life, remember it so desolate?
I see you as beautiful flowers that dance.
And at 53 years I feel I would long to have your flowers spread my field
You are not my conqueror–I invite you to come
I am not prey–you bring no violence
You are not prey–I bring craftless transparent hands
You are not hunter–you bring only flowers
We bring no tools of our profession–we bring only open hands and an unfurled beating heart
And as I look at your open hands, as I look at your beating heart, as I look at you, sweet flower that dances, your roots stretch past my eyes and run past my hands.
Your roots find my heart and take root there.
And as your roots interleave with my heart, an army of buds appear within me, buds of yellow, of transparency, of dancing
And I wonder, were Adam and Eve so blessed, as to feel the same budding and blossoming and hope and joy
And we dance, we dance, in this field of possibilities. We dance in this field of buds and hopes and dreams
God of Jesus and Love, please flourish this budding so only everyone can only ever see that you budded in us.
Oh God, strip away all pretence and convention and useless blinding hiding words.
Oh God of the lost lamb and of the forever and who loved even the lost Adam, so keep us always found in each other, discovering freshly and delighting anew
Oh God of the caterpillar-become-butterfly, begin your transformation in our hearts that we always grow closer to you and then to each other–to You first, knowing that you always create the symphony that joins to our duet, our small melodies joining to your greater melodic sound, your more marvellous deeper eternal anthem.

Chapter 61
THE SECRET

Oh God, always show us the
truth about ourselves, then
work on us to refine us.

In Your name
Amen.

Chapter 62
KATHY REFLECTS

    He struggles, he prays, "Lord, show me the truth about me, so I can lay down before you what is not of You."
So painful a prayer.
And he changes, we change. Daring the unknown, setting aside old old evils that have lurked yet as present in our habits and actions and mannerisms and demeanours.
Such a prayer to pray–how non-easy to see yourself as with warts and squints and uncontrolled falls (whether to the external or internal world), to see like false captains the movements we do instinctively to protect or conceal ourselves.
He is a bird with broken wings, never knowing the sky.
But yes!
One more hour with him!
I will always be asking this knight for one more hour.

Chapter 63
GREG'S NERVOUS 4AM WAIT FOR KATHY FOR A BEACH WALK

The world prickles me. The sun rises, pushes its way into my senses

I love you, I want you and yet I am anxious. I love our road. I love how your breath intermingles with mine as we come close to kiss. The heat in my heart offers hopes and calms.

The sun lazily hugging the horizon. And I leave my house to find you, to walk the beach together as the sun eases up the sky. As the clean air of morning rises upon the Gold Coast, I enjoy, I anticipate a possible deeper moment that will cover all our lives

I seek you as I turn the corner, shuffling the fresh fallen dew that falls before the heat of the day

I walk in symphony and prickles. I push through the wet grass with melody and edginess. I walk with you in the early morning

I know over the past months there is so much change inside me. I am becoming. Before God, I am recovering from a world of caring that collapsed.

But there are shards inside

me.

Shards by history and shards by mis-remembering and shards by mistaken well-meaning design

****

    Ever only
    Yours,
    O God Who sees

Chapter 64
GREG, IN FEAR OF REJECTION, GOING INWARDS

There is in me a blind spot.
When you look a little distant at me, I feel fear. Perhaps back pain, perhaps the leaving–my mind thinks both...
Will you reject me?
I slide to blue and inward.
So inward that I can not reach you over the distance
I could get lost in here
And so I have to focus that I will give to you regardless of what you give or don't give me.
Somehow that eases the fear, eases the pressure–and there's space, there's room to feel free to fly again with you
In loving you unconditionally, I fly free

****

Boats bob gently, tugging their cords
Your heart tugs gently, taking my all
My feet long always to share your path
Your kiss, your hopes are my joy, my warmth

Chapter 65
THE TWO, AMONG THE AUNTS, DANCE INSIDE

My eyes stay on you, my love, even as we enter the restaurant.

I am 48, my love, and I thought I would never know a breath like you, never thought I would hold hands with a gentle fighter, never thought I would know this moment when I would enter with you to find my waiting relatives.

Dancing together forever in our hearts, as we find the table.

They rise to meet us, her mum and aunts and aunts' friends.

"So good to finally see..." "Kathy told us so much..." "So good to get to know a little..." "Oh, such a lovely lovely place..."

And we sit amidst a huddle of aunts and perfume. I catch her eye, and we signal phrases with our gaze, although we talk of weather and The Broadwater, of family and news and roads and old meetings.

"So so interesting how you met..."

And we tell the beautiful story again, shaping each moment even now, though it was two months ago.

And I think: how will you cope, my knight, with the pressing in of perfume and questions, with voice piled upon voice upon excitement? And you, my aunts, as we sit hand in hand, how will you view our first hands in public before you? (So momentous!)

"Toowoomba is such a pretty place. I passed through there in March. The flowers were so beautiful. We found a park there and walked through it. The breeze was cool and bracing; but the sun still won out..."

Year upon year, longing to introduce my love to those so special to me. How do you see us, my dear dear ones?

"Yes, the Carnival there is such a beautiful thing. I've always planned to go. They used to show it on the news, even here on the Gold Coast. And there were so many gardens to explore in the late afternoon. We really should all go..."

You are spark and heat and fire, you are the supplied in His giving, you are presented and here with me–my heart squeezes that you are, all of a sudden, so here.

"Tell us about your family. Do you have any brothers or sisters? Your mother, is she alive still? Have you always lived in Queensland? And was it always in the country..."

Their face so lit up with joy and excitement as we had entered, and still so so here. I am excitement, I am anxiety, and I am your companion, and we will always run together into our life adventure.

"What shall we eat? I remember the last time they cooked a wonderful meal. Now, can I recall? Yes, it was a..."

And as we sit, my heart turns on your words of love. After you, freedom is both impossible and already completely attained. Hold my heart grip in your heart—you give it existence. In your eyes I see myself as new.

And you, O God, you are Creator. Create us now and in every kiss.

And a blizzard of dishes and questions asked of my love, questions piling up in excitement, of smiles and reminiscing, of histories and commonalities, of cousins and cousins' cousins and shared times in other cities, although years apart.

The food touching forks touching mouths, the dancing waves surfing the dancing water.

Late afternoon sun kissing the dust motes in the chattering air and the symphony of warmth of sun and fellowship in the room.

Farewells and goodbyes and smiles and hands.

And later, texts and joy and phones and voices... "He is lovely... So gentle a gentleman... How nice the meeting... Yes, new acquaintances, new connections..."

...and the coalescing of new common paths.

The excitements in my soul, my love, at 48. Forty-eight, and I finally

                                                finally get to say,

"This is my love, my aunts; come, come meet him..."

****

        So, your finger here, my palm just there
        They fit so well, your hand and mine
        We turn to kiss, our hands squeeze tight
        Never did something earthly feel so right

Chapter 66
THE TWO EXPERIMENT IN TRUST

The burble of broken jigsaw pieces sliding into place. You pull me from me, from introspection, from the fallen dream.

You bring me dancing to replace my despair, the upward path from morass and swamp.

You have taught me breathing.

Remember when we'd known each other just weeks. We were heading into the shopping centre, and you turned to me and squeezed my hand, "Trust me?"

And I did, very much, except for where I hadn't.

And you said, "Trust me? Close your eyes."

And I closed, and held your hand, and we walked slowly–you into the shopping centre, and I with you, into the dark

Trusting–the experiment ending safely.

Deeper and deeper always, my love.

****

> Lean into me. I love your soul,
> Hear your heart, feel your chest expand
> My head on your chest, Our hopes entwine
> Hold me my love until th' sun flees earth

Chapter 67
HOT LONGING NIGHTS

Fevered I lie, dear woman, and think of you...

You my sweetheart...

You sleeping less than two blocks away,

                                        are you lying there...

lying there awake

                like me...

Lying there, looking at the lonely impartial moon, longing for heat that is not sun–the heat that burns far too brightly for mere suns?

Do you rise, your night clothes clinging slightly to your thigh, so that, so that you reach to touch it, to correct it–and in that instant think of me and if I were there and the blaze that would ignite
and at the window, you bite at your lip, your beautiful soft lip
So now I
        I, your knight, rise
                now
        rise in a cruel universe that has you nowhere near me.
I resolve…
        …I will survive a sleepless night to hold you pure.

But don't let them say it's easy. Don't let the idiots and pious speakers say they conquer and fly through clouds of grace, of God's sustaining power.

This surging is as dynamite, this rampart and building and climbing and erection is from deep within the psyche, this yearning forest fire has been shaping and defining of all my years since puberty, this is fire and I burn in every city I visit for even a night. I survive with God, just with God.

You who sleep in your bed near your wife, your well of which you drink deeply and sleep contentedly, you cannot imagine thirty-five years of raging inferno, raging forever, burning forever, except for the rigidly muted acknowledgement and build and rest)….

Can you imagine surviving this, you smoothsayer? Imagine thirty-five years of the fire and clinging to God, of the fire and escaping? (And as I write this, I realise how much, how much indeed, the thirty-five years buckling has buckled me.)

I have not broken, but there is the buckled tilted neurotic fire–have not broken knowing that God is near, and the temptation will never storm the wall to breaking, that God will bring me through this fiery flood as through flames
as if one driven and running and trusting him.

Write your words carefully, moral do-gooders who say this is easy… This is fire and singing, flood and raft clinging, prayer and agony

You, who married at 22, you have no knowledge. Mute your mouth.

                ****

        Be my fire and my dance.
        Last breath together, then we kiss and part
        Our hearts still together as we say
        I yearn! Come quick, tomorrow's dawn!

                ****

        Adore you gorgeous heart, gorgeous soul

Poetically Together

You are near and yes I triumph
You are far, I deeply yearn
For just some seconds of your beauty near
The heady wine of your beautiful soul

Your kiss deep delights my soul
A soul so full of clack and hum
I revel in our nearness times
Though to my soul you are always near

Naysayers may put us down
Cast a net at our eagle wings
Foretell our defeat, our fall ahead
O God, build us: lovers and friends.

Chapter 68
THE TWO DO IKEA

We kiss and pack...
...coffee and food and her back support into the car
Beat your heart next to me all my life, my love. Breathe your life always in my hearing.
...we sing badly to our shared shared songs.
We sing loudly, uncaring–for to each other it sounds like joy caressing air. We sing without pretence–and we seek no pretence. Whether we cry or sob or run or shout, be you (and I so long that it always will be the true you I see.)
Arrive at Ikea at sunset, and bundle in through the door, camera and excitement and...
    the other so near

We walk the aisles
   we walk and dream

We talk of ideas and joys and plans and futures. We learn of each other, from each other, by each other. And dear one, I have learned I love you without fear. I am safe without walls here with you as our dreams shove out the neutral air.

Greg and Kathy Weller

And if we were to marry, the kitchen

                                             ah the kitchen

I long to create a kitchen, shape a kitchen and a future.... with you, my love, with you. I cannot hear the old me for the two we are.

Imagine we up in the morning
                 to this
                             Or perhaps this here

Yes yes, the brown
                 the brown tiles on the floor, cold, stinging our feet a little
and loving it
                 and being it.

The house like this, that lounge hugging the corner ... or perhaps maybe diagonal.

We are two, we are children, we are near middle age, we are beginners. Let the world have its brutes and its takers and its liars and its catfishers. But you, my love, are here. The world never touches us here.

And to the cupboards and laid out ensuite

                 and move this here
and that over there
                 and tables
                 and containers

             and the desk
                   adjustable legs!

And I am almost out of body in wonderment—is this real, is this here and touching me?

Are you boundary-breaker, are you my raft in floods, are you my knight and life-sharer?

Poetically Together

For over 30 years, I have dreamed you, longed these things, hugged the pillow hugging you. I have dreamed our walking hand in hand, walking in transparency,
as as
as giraffe, no wall ever constructed to keep the other's eyes out.

as spies out of work, for all our needful facts are laid nudely bare

as carers and lovers, no rescuers

And the buying of a desk
for our future

> We have
> come
> by car
> to dream
> to walk
> to do the things that, for some, ignite argument and fire
>
> but we walk
> here
> in
> a beautiful
> hopeful
>
> sweet sweet
> time.

This at 48!

> And we arrived and kissed at sunset at the entry
> And we live our last kiss in the dark, in our last song
> We are love without law, we are passion that burns in lines.
> We are adults and pure
>
> Ikea a distant long-term dream now real

We kiss goodbye—to each their home.

****

> I love you and cradle your head in love
> Embrace your eyes, such showing of souls
> Melt reserve, melt composure and doubt
> "Here's my soul," my eyes call out

Chapter 69
GREG REVELS IN HIS WOMAN

Your beauty comes in an avalanche; you tumble me from myself. You tumble me so that down is no longer a meaningful direction.

You unfurl my heart and all my hopes.

I step out under a sun of love. You have shown me a new land of swooping valleys and mountain peaks, of plains long and fertile, of the sky that kisses the earth. I would dance with you in the soft dewy grass, kiss your mouth in the flooding rain, would walk with you any way you would go, and toy with your fingers in the evening nightfall as the night closes its cozy grasp.

You burn fires in me, discover the new in me. There was a butterfly - who knew? There was a song - an early morning speech deep in the throat as the ocean dances its promise of our everywhere-Creator and everyloving-Jesus.

Hand in hand, heart in heart, passion cradled in patience in passion.

The every breathing of your breath near me this early morning

****

> You drop allure
> The evening falls to its knees

Chapter 70
GREG ASKS KATHY'S DAD FOR PERMISSION

Walking carefully through wet grass and truth.

How to say it?

To take a look back at the last three months, perhaps a "Sir" and then the allowing of time for pondering, for his weighing the question.

And I watch you, my knight, from the distance, from the park, where my mother and I wander in waiting.

There was to be a gentle stepping into it, a respectful tone, a knowing that she had come from his genetic mix, from this man that I walked beside.

Future danced in the phrasing. The method simply the asking, the non-ploy, the non-lie, just the vulnerable time and the asking...

To ask

To ask his permission

And I watch these men. Two men so opposite who walk together. My father so so impatient–so coffee gulp, so gone. So work as rush, the site left at speed.

And my love–so methodical, so slow with detail in his thoughts and moves. They walk, two opposites, two rhythms, two deciders.

And I remind myself I mustn't forget the Sir in the second part of the speech. Perhaps one, perhaps more...

"So," I breathe and push words into this moment of waiting, "Well, I've got to know your wonderful daughter over the last three months, and..."

"Greg, if you're asking what I think you're asking, the answer's Yes."

"Oh...

          "...um, pardon, Sir?"

"The answer is <u>Yes</u>."

"Thank you, Sir. Thank you. That's excellent news."

Greg's relaxation of breathing

My love, the detail man.
My father,
my father,
        Whom no one can keep up with
        In his bustle and speed

My men
In their walking

Greg pausing

Pause
More breathing
Dad: "Will we go back and re-join the girls?"
"Sounds good" \<relief and smile\>

Pause

"Umm, just checking.... It's the worse of being a QA Manager, lol... When you said, 'The answer is Yes,' you meant
My men, still talking.
My mum in impatience. "What's taking them so long?"
"Yes, that I could marry your daughter?"
"Yes, Greg" A sigh and smile.
"What are these men doing? Why so long?"
And Greg smiled, "That is so so excellent."
And we were back with the girls.
And my love, I know that you dotted any "i" and crossed any "t" and found the details all correct. How I love you, my love!
And I touch her hand.

I touch the future and its shared pillow under our weary heads.

Chapter 71
KATHY'S LOVE

So many things I had not thought to ask God for in a man, so many things I had not thought to ask God to allow me, so many things I had not dreamed to ask for they all came wrapped up in you.

Our fingers intertwine in desperate love, your arms are a light house, your hand is a harbour in which I could drop anchor to only spend all my life with you. Hand in hand, for each our harbour, soul with soul sharing entangled anchors beneath the still and smiling sky.

You have earned all my trust—my plans are all open to you. There are no secrets.

Within the stones of my heart, flowers bloom. You create a fire upon my breath and in my heart. You sing me like Solomon did. May my melody of Eve rise to meet you, my dearest man.

All my old books of blackness and sadness and longing and despair are forgotten, are burned, they have fled away.

And similarly, my beloved, as I encourage you towards emotion without rejection, as we journey to a whole other world of connection with ourselves and others, may God hold our garden and ebb away our old worlds and grant us peace

Poetically Together

May He grant us peace

****

> I cuddle you so so close
> In the family photograph pose
> My heart and soul, body and mind
> call to you so close "I love you,"
> call even through silence and static pose

Greg and Kathy Weller

MELODY

RUSHES

TO

CRESCENDO

Greg and Kathy Weller

Chapter 72
GREG IS NERVOUS ABOUT HOW SERIOUS IT IS GETTING

Morning and
I rejoice that I know you
I scare that I know you

You make void my defences
Yet defences I never knew within me
Spring up yet again.

Yet I anticipate
One day I'll stretch my hand
And find you there.
One day I'll feel you breathe
My bedroom air
And it will be heaven
When I wake
And find
Find you defenceless and waking

But the room falls dark in corners sometimes...
And I scare...

What if you are devourer
What if there is the unknown in you
What if you are not you
And unfurl your evil after "I do".

And I hand my anxiety to God

But there is always the whisper in my head
Of deep shadows, of deep acts upon an imagined time

I look in your eyes

Greg and Kathy Weller

    I find love
    I feel your soul
       It beats Christ's
    I have never found a
        lamb of a woman
            as defenceless as you
                kind as you
                    fitting to my soul and spirit
                              None like you.

But are you you?
The whisper stands unanswered
    In this morning light
I stumble to breakfast
    And the sober outside light.

Chapter 73
THE TWO DO THAI

We walk in
                      our hands signalling love
              our hearts singing and full

                                          the steam from the kitchen
                                          the singing of oil and wok

          we walk in
               eyes to each other
         as they steer us to a table

                                          the room dimmed
                                        the candle dances our souls

And I say we are proximal and sagittal and lateral–in all ways our love and longing and being surrounds the other, surrounds each other and sets us free.

                we hold the other's hand

Poetically Together

                      across the table
and ask deep questions

                Look, here is my soul
                Show me yours
      and the laugh
      the hand squeeze

Food arrives, and we
      part hands
      but never our souls

We are changing day on day, week on week. We become the fliers, we become the feathered diving in grace.

                We eat
                and ginger tickle–
                the crisp beef a delight
      Dessert
      Always you, my love
      Dessert comes

      but I am already full

                            your eyes
                            your dancing eyes.

Chapter 74
THE TWO SEEK TO COMMUNICATE AND CHANGE

"What is that thing that needs to change in me?"
We breathe this to each other.
We breathe this to God.

We ask the three questions... What have I done this week that made you feel good? What have I done this week that hurt you? What is something you would like me to change?

We listen with hearts so suddenly beating their fear. We listen and clarify, careful as jewellers. We understand, we thank, we walk away, we process.

We don't defend, we don't attack. We ask till we understand, we thank politely, we walk away.

We process.

And we have freedom to change or not change. We have freedom to change in love. We have freedom to refuse and the other accepts that freedom.

And if we are honest with ourselves (each in the quiet corner of room and of mind), we then bring that love and gift to the other.

And when we find our blind spot, in the area we would rather not go, in that place where the lightest slip could lead to tumble, we say and we are vulnerable and we lean into the other and say we

we don't know

and for that there is help. For that there is counselling, for that there is a counsellor.

And if we call, "This is too big a place", then in that place there is love and acceptance and a searching for a mechanism for coping or for change or for compromise or for occasional excess.

Truth can be so hard to understand in truth and depth.

And God will always honour the heart that hugs the truth. There will be an answer.

FOR MORE DISCUSSION AND EXAMPLES OF THE THREE QUESTIONS SEE APPENDIX ONE (RIGHT AT THE BACK OF THE BOOK)

Chapter 75
THE TWO SEEK THEIR GOALS

We revel that we have left our baggage.
                            So far as is possible, we
                            have left our baggage.

            Oh, how the loop could spin
                  generation upon generation
            "This was my parents' pattern."
            "This was my teenage pattern."
            "This was my relationship pattern."
            "This was my fear and rejection pattern."
And you would act, and I would respond
            As an echo of patterns I would respond
                Old pattern, old action, old consequence...

But you at the teenage camp
and I every day with conscious step

      Pray
      We pray "God, show us the truth
      About us
      About faults
      About sin and the brokenness
      About rejection and depression
      About the learnt ... to be unlearnt

      And then, O God,
      Work in us to leave it behind
      Place us in situations
      Cover us in circumstances
      Circumstances where holding onto what's right
            (To what Scriptures urges), leads to a fight
            knowing that repeated new actions
            new attitudes, relying on God and prayer

Lead slowly, inexorably to a re-shaping
of the mind.
It is hard, it is pain, it is white-knuckle, it
is God-actioned
And He will bring us through.

And to move to Scriptural wife, adorned of beautiful spirit
And to move to Scriptural husband,
who echoes the Christ of Philippians 2
These our aims! These our goals!

And if we are unknowing, unsure, there is counselling,
      there is advice, there is the second opinion

But only only when combined with prayer

****

Forever dancing with you in my heart,
My embraceable, my other breath!
I feel so alive as our company ends;
I fall to sleep—then relive joy again!

Chapter 76
THE GONDOLA

And to you, my captain, I give our gondola.

You are my love, my captain—though it may not be true for others, it works for me. You are my knight. You protect me at the risk of your own hurt.

The water before us splashes down carelessness spreading over gravity. It loses its bounds in our unseeing and in the bounds of the night.

I cannot explain happiness but it is you. I can't measure delight, but my delight sways and spreads like this limitless water. We surge towards marriage. We are coastguards who rescued each other. We are fever this wistful Spring Gold Coast night.

And these swelling waves chop and rock, slightly impatient and wild.

Poetically Together

Your tides are in my heart, my love, my heart's ship you pull to deepness. You bring me so close, closer than undertow. We reach, we clip our towline into Him and each other. We pull our companions–and are pulled.

And together as one, we will set sail this tiny boat this perfect night, touch the sunset who pours paint on this ocean, romance into every wave and rise

Such hard work to find our gondola!
>> so much research
>> and slowly
>> so slowly
>> the finding
>> the finding of
>> a tiny boat, a driver outside the cabin,
>> a beautiful meal in romance

>> our boat caressing, sailing lightly, the Broadwater

>> our boat, our date, was found
>> the call, the booking

so excited, so excited.

>>>>>>> (The expense,
>>>>> but no matter.)

The giving, the gift, to my man, in sincerity
>>> to God who bought him here
>>> to newness (the sun no longer sent to bed, weeping)
>>> to rest, to a symphony that sings my soul
>>> to new moments in the new better normal

>>> (My love, how have you taken reality and
>>>>>> re-clothed it
>>>>>> you re-clothe it
>>>>>> in
>>>> new yellows
>>>> and reds
>>>> and joys
>>>> and vibrance

                and heat
                            that is you.

    How did you change everything?
           even my old desert and brute sun
           even the old silences that crushed down on my heart

    You have carried my heart from pallid to red.
    On Earth, these stones (my heart) can sing.)
    The water goes away from my eyes.

And here, my captain, the gondola dancing solid waves.
Dancing as gift, dancing as kisses upon your soul.
                        And I kiss too your beauty,
                                  your lips
                                        sweet sweetness

    I have dreamt this gift to you, you who have spread fragrance across this soul this night.

    From your relatives (first meeting) and cautious dance and etiquette and impressions to...

    ...to our gondola, our hearts adrift on words of love.

    We step into the boat like stepping onto skate boards of delight. *O how you light up my life,* and the night hugs us, tells secrets between us and the water

    The hot pot with meal in front of us *and you are sweetness and breath, my beloved, my woman...*

    The pilot up front, muted and away–and there is only us in this seasalt moment *I am overcome, have no words to lay before you, my love* and he sets his oars into the water the rocking water the slow flowing slightly out of control water, the water like fever, and slowly around the Broadwater, we slowly surrounding the Broadwater like you have surrounded my heart... *and how the world is washed away as wreckage.* The dipping in of the oars, like the tugging of hearts that always brings me closer to you. Day by day so closer so so closer

    We eat the meal–and like this moment it is rare and beautiful and only us. Only us, my love. *I love you.* And we kiss–and there is all the stars in it *and the world is castaway. There is only love.*

Chapter 77
KATHY THRILLS

My heart turns on your words of love
We rise up to our whirlwind, our music, and our choices. Everything in moderation– oh, we believe that also applies to moderation

May we never know less than love–nor, by action or inaction, seek less than the other's unequalled joy.

Your kisses fall me into this moment–and I am caught by you and heaven

My love, dearest heart, let me be the stream in which you find genuineness, honesty and ever unrequited giving.

And if today we die, in love we still come to tomorrow. The edge of love tinctures gold leaf on each moment of this day.

Chapter 78
GREG HAS JITTERY NERVES ABOUT THEIR FUTURE TOGETHER

Stay my heart, still your qualms
Are we not within loving caring palms
The threat to falter, to stumble, to fall
Is tiny compared to His yearning call

Chapter 79
KATHY KNOWS UNKNOWING

This is spring and almost summer.
We are whirlwind and singing. We are those who are, for each other. We sing and sacrifice, we dare and thrill the whirlwind, we hug the other slowly amidst the warm coastal nights.
We hold the world in this moment, in this hour, in this day.
That you love me folds down into my soul a thousand roses, ten thousand lutes, a myriad of scattering doves…
And a fear

We surge in the whirlwind…
                                  we surge surges of fear
                                  amid surges of our laughter
                                  amid the surges of

the future finding
its presence now in
in the breath between us

This is almost summer.
                              I step and splash, the little girl,
                              All the fountains and puddles of love
                              Scattered me around
                              There is love like floods
                                and summer rains and drenching

This is almost war end
                              War and fighting and sorrow
                              The chains I held around me,
                              Amidst the chains that really chained
                              They are let go loose near my feet
                              There is freedom like laughter
                                and singing and evening guitar

This is almost found

Poetically Together

              We have found each other
              I long for your warm cheek on mine,
              for the closing of our eyes as we nestle
                each other,
                feel each other's warmth...

But there is my fear, my recurrent fear
My back so injured,
So much time off work

And I
And I
       scare.
So often it has stopped me, so often the days at work fled away, so often friends left alone, so often the event left unattended

And to you, my passion singer, I say: what if I am like this all our life's fire, what if I find that life together becomes life as cared and carer, what if I fall to your resentment and wondering?

What if future and holders become clouds and the beholden?

What if… What if…

but

But I whisper no. Life must not be "what if". "What if's" bring life to prison, and I'll not be locked down.

No! In vulnerable terror and innocence, I pray… then I touch you and pour out my fear. I fly as kites all my sensitivities, hold as frailty and frailty-while-loved all my hopes and life and dreams.

And in that God-call and holding, and then fiancé-call and holding, I become safe.

No matter the future, I am safe.

No matter the sickbed or daybed or crutches or tension, I am safe.

Hoping no expectation, but that God is loving-God and gracing-God and fervent-God and fervent-love, I am safe.

We are safe.
You and I and God are multiple, becoming safe.

And in the dark, we know the secret to light; in pain-grip, we know the love-grip of God and the other.

And if my body is caught in a thicket of thorns, if my body malingers its bed despite the klaxon call, if my body brings me shame and I turn and cry, if little movements become the too too big things for me, I do not need to challenge God, "Pick a side,"
  for He is _for_ me.
He is always knowing
         and holding
and supplying the right next minute
and even for you my love
while pain and painkiller may
        quell my pain ... and me
        sing pain to sleep ... and me
        rest down my pain ... and me
He still will hold you.
Soon we seek marriage,
(It seems, it surely seems)
And exactly married, we will be One
Despite this cutting-edge bed,
Despite the murder of all our dreams
He will still hold us

                  There is spring and romance in our air
                  There are dreams of the music
                  Canon in D as I walk as I walk the sands
                  I walk the sands to you–
                  Our beach front wedding
                  And the holding of hands before them all
                  Before heart guests and hushing birds
                  And the waves that brush gently the future
                  Brush gently the sorrows and tears away

And then I awake
There was sleep and no pain–
Amidst red eyes and corruption
        There was no pain and a resting.

Chapter 80
GREG REFLECTS ON KATHY'S SORE BACK

Everyday we joy to craft beauty.
Everyday seeds grow and blossom and bear fruit.
But your back crafts its own will and rebellion, sends you to bed, sends you to pain and tablets
My love and companion, you are my love, and I will help. You are heartbeat and beauty and fallen.
I reach with the liniment on your back, longing to soothe the pain and ease your soul, to bring you coffee and longing, attention and commitment.
Fly again soon, my heart's keeper. In my mind you are ever in my arms.

Chapter 81
KATHY RESPONDS

My world is a world I once never knew:
Brightness, laughter, remarkable love,
Having a man of God near, so deep and true.
God made me rich, first with Jesus, then YOU!

Chapter 82
THE TWO GIFT A FRIEND

My dear friend, my bosom friend...
Together we saw bears.
And you have rung me at all your foundations: at engagement, at weddings, at the blossoming news of pregnancy.
How often we two have been hand in hand: hand in hand with joy, hand in hand with the gasp and sorrow; hand in hand with the bottom out of our worlds, with black bears and dogs that came across the slippery ice...

And today, my friend, today, we two celebrate you.

After all our waiting years, we celebrate you…
And so, we two up…
…to go to a skating rink dressed as Canadians and sing the Canadian National anthem, to videotape it and send it you, my dear Canadian friend.
We into motion!

The music downloaded. We test it.
It spills into the room in French!
But no time to waste, no time to waste!!
Grab the stuffed toy moose, the heavy jackets. Tonight outside is a Gold Coast summer, but Canadians are never warm.
Grab the Canadian blankets–the letters of the nation in large white letters across the red blanket
Spill into the car with ipad and speaker and camera and joy
Spill out the car at the skating rink
Sudden cold feet… "Maybe we shouldn't go in? Maybe just sing it in the carpark?"
And we laugh and position ourselves ready
And French words sing world-friendship to the nearby building
We are pierced by peering as others walk by
But no matter. We raise the standard high
We sing deeply to the stuffed moose
We check the video
Done!
Excellent!!

Back in the car laughing.

Chapter 83
THE HOURS

And I say to you, as your doctor, that there is no knowing. Your back falls apart and hurts you. But you have each other and there is strength, there will be strength.

There is heart in you both that hungers, there in soul in you both that yearns still and struggles. There is strength. Even when your back falls apart and hurts you both, there will be strength.

Your back knots up at the slightest thing, it feels pain, and somehow the pain spreads and runs, and little knots of hardness and swelling and pain ripple and spread their kingdoms.

"Massage two, three times a day. When the pain runs to knots, coax away the knots, work the knots slowly–if they are moved whilst soft, before the swellings harden, there is relief.

"Here–let me write a script."

And at her home, the labour of love.

So often, the labour of love...

….. and the easing to longer active days.

Chapter 84
GREG COMMITS WITHOUT KNOWING THE FUTUREFALL

And if I am never to most deeply know you in touch, knowing you here in this fever is enough.

As knight after knight to antiquity, I supply your hope and need, my Lady.

As jester and strongman and wrestler and servant, I assert my labour.

I ask nothing. Love for you lays at your door. The cost is not too much...

    ... not much at all.

Chapter 85
THE TWO SEARCH AND FIND

Time calls us! Briefly we run to the northern beaches, my love, my woman!

And we recall, just so recent, the finding of manuka-honey nuts. We both had tasted ... and they were good. And Greg knew they were from the big, big grocery chain.

And as we travel north, Greg promising himself to bring delight, to bringing to her more of the beautiful taste, everytime he saw the store, he would urge to, "Pull over, pull over, they're going to be here!"

And we two out of the car and in the door, hand in hand and breathless, looking for the nuts, down the aisle, finding the place, bending to look, stretching in hope, looking– and out the door, vowing it was the next one.

And the gentle asking, her gentle asking: could it possibly be the other big grocery chain, and Greg insisting, "No, it's definitely... Definitely... We'll find it. The next one'll be it."

and on, and on.

Still further, still on...

...and soon, Greg says, "Hey, maybe we should try the other one. It might just be the other one, though of course it isn't."

And we out of the car, so close to the holiday place, running out of time to find the new taste, and we up, out of the car tired and wanting, and in through the unfamiliar doors (after trying the other chain in fifteen towns), and down the aisle, and look dispirited and still hoping, and

find it

find it

fifteen stores all wrong, memory all wrong, humanly so, so mistaken

And so right

And the breaking open of the packet in the car

And the enjoying

And the squeezing of the other's hand.

Poetically Together

Chapter 86
GREG RESOLVES HIS ACTIONS

And the Christ that gave away everything to become man, the Christ that gave away being a man to become the captive, the Christ that gave away no freedom to become no living thing–may my actions, and the actions of each and every man, reflect that to their betrothed, their companion, their hand-held heart-held one. May they reflect this giving, this love, this making of one's needs and rights to become of no account.

Chapter 87
KATHY REJOICES

The future were so unlimited had we met when we were young; the future so so more unlimited now that we are real

                     real and known

and now.

Chapter 88
THE TWO DO THE COMEDY CLUB

Greg so proud–

    It was almost impossible to find anything,

He prayed and searched,

                  phoned and researched,

      And yes!
      At last yes!
    HOTA Comedy club

It <u>had</u> been so strange–the seating plan

Greg and Kathy Weller

                The back seats full
          The front rows empty
                                        But yes!
                                        the best seats
                                        (the front seats)
                                        reserved and paid

      So we up,
      I and he up
      Leave my home
      We up
      Up and with the same shirt
      One for him, one for me
      And we wear them on
                              our bodies
      The matching tee
              The logo "Not Normal"
        the picture: an idiot of a duck
      And we out and lock the door
      The car—and in!

So proud—she had had no idea where we were going.
And the telling and the surprise, the surprise.

      We reach the comedy club, he and I
      And I remember
      Our first emails
      Joke after joke after giggle after laugh
      And so I knew
            This would be a special place for him and me.

      And we entered the back door
      We walked

      We walked
                And I a little concerned
                "These seats? These seats here?"

Poetically Together

And Greg in his T-shirt smiled and nodded.
                The front seats
                Fronted, centred
                He and I sit

                I gulp
                In the too-bright darkness I gulp
                And look at my man

The two sat
And
The show began
                And out comes the MC
                Comic and skilled
                              the room on board
                And seeing us, the question
                to Greg, "What's your name?"

And Greg responds
                as he always does
                as he processes and responds -
                                "Er, Greg"

                The comedian:
                "Arr Greg. Arr Greg, the pirate.

                "And who's this?"

                "Arr my girl, Kathy."

                "She your girl, pirate Greg?"

                "Yes"
                              And the asking, thankfully briefly, of
                                    Too many, too long the questions

Greg and Kathy Weller

                                            and another joke

              and he away

                    found someone else
                            Greg suddenly realising
                            the seats
                            had been
                            untaken
                            deliberately...

                  There was perhaps a reason
                        <u>no-one</u>
                  had booked the front seats.

And a spotlight
On us, T-shirts "Not normal"
Showed to, shouted the club,
We were never
      Could never be
                normal

We
beautiful to each other as mountain lakes
disarming to each other as seals in love
sweet to each other as kiwifruit in fall
hearts hugging the other's day
as water to the other's thirst

as singers
as loving
as telling

but

never
no, never
normal

****

My kisses be upon your lips
Like flowers of petalled love.

Chapter 89
GREG STRUGGLES

I believe, I try to believe
    The seconds of doubt slide to minutes
    Then sweatily back to calm

I believe in fervent.
I believe that God reaches down.
I believe He is passionate and shaping
He is proactive, never waiting.
A quick prayer to Him (He who is *always* there)

        And He is working
        He is up and bringing
        His perfect will to be

He is the One I allow to change me
He is the One I allow total control
I have been as pebbles
Was once, at one time
        A strong rock, once iron...
        Shattered–me, yes me–I am pebbles
        Muddered and splattered and ground.

In soul and emotion and body
I have torn myself apart
        For my mother

To keep her living
To keep her smiling
To bear her up gently to her grave.

She died well!, and it is me
Who lives only because He lives
I believe Him and choose to act whole
          because I believe He is psychologist
                            and builder
                            and keeper
                            and flightmaker

I believe

I believe that in your hurt, my love,
I believe that in your broken body and my broken soul,
there is God, and His action,
there is His unending grace and delight,
His proactive yearning within our trauma and struggle and pain.

And so
And so
And so I
        breathe

And so I plan a date
A date within our limits and days

And so I calm
And so I step out
                to find you
                to hold you
                to step beside you
                the journey that He makes.

Chapter 90
THE TWO WANT...

Together this song!

Together this hymn!

Together to bring this joy!

Together to talk the world of Jesus!

Together, a Christian marriage,
Together a Christian voice,
Together seeking to be most purely
(Although we slip and fall
So there is mud on our face
So there is the stench of fallibility
And sin and falling on our hands)...

...seeking most purely,
in our weakness and our repentance and our return to falling,

to be ever only God's.

and to tell the world,

                even if we are the

                              lone
                              voice
                              singing.

Chapter 91
KATHY STRUGGLES THE NEGATIVE PREDICTIONS OF THEIR FUTURE

All the relatives and friends
    Lie as thieves at my door,
Talking of reality and
    How it washes love to dust,
    How it stumbles hearts to rust.

I look in your eyes, my love,
And a surer love spurs me on.

Chapter 92
KATHY RESOLVES

I choose to walk, no fear–
Reality, not "what if."
Reality is God.
Reality is
        you and me
        here with your eyes
        and your breathing.

Chapter 93
GREG SLIDES–AND RECOVERS

And in the dark times
The pulse yawns a chasm,

And I think, I am a fool;
I can't entwine with you

I cannot give you my years
        And my heart
        (So many fears, so many layers,
        Murked and pooled as heavy heavy oil
        Pooling till they rise like floods
                Upon a desperate soul
              (I can't swim, I can't swim))

But everytime

Everytime

Everytime this flood comes,
the shuffled ipod that pushes into this heavy room
Switches to

        to the

        to the same song

Look of Love starts
        Starts and plays again

And I stop and breathe

        Eight times as the flood rises around my feet
        And shoes lose their grip

Eight times as the dread rises
>And I would flee

Eight times as I wonder
>the dread dread question, "Dare I?"

Eight times
>these past few months

Eight times
The ipod turned to that tune

Perfect timing,
>Perfect God.

Chapter 94
KATHY DAYDREAMS THE FUTURE

It will affect my world like bells.
It will come. He will kneel, no deceit no pretence, and invite me into his boat, into his world, into his painted and dramatic and methodical and pounding-so-loud-this-crazy-music boat, into his world
And he will pause, the implicit RSVP
>and I will be in that giving moment–
>>the moment that God bends and places in my hands, my trembling hands, the loss of years of pain, the loss of the sureness that no one would come, the loss of the lingering and bitter and onrushing loss of tears and the stretching never-ending Sunday afternoon ... and the too too still Saturday night and

>and I will "Yes."
>I will look to him, look in his eyes. And we two lovers and callers and humans-become-human would waltz the moon, would whirl and dance and sing, would bring the precious moment, would
>>hold

Poetically Together

    hold
    hold the moment as a ring glinting in the moonlight
    hold hands that squeeze, telegraphing our hearts
    (we squeeze to telegraph quietly our love while our hearts
                                       semaphore
                                         and thump
                                         and joy
                                         and rejoice

                  rejoice
                  at the
                  finding)
and I know, I know
        someday we will be falling,
        someday we will be plucked away
        someday we will be into the storm's rage
                      but together
                      in the terror moment
                      always together
                            ... and I say
                            I only want you
                            I only want you there
and then we would kiss
I would taste his kiss
        (how his lip is the bowl of his beautiful heart's words)

And I would lean
        lean into him
        and breathe the evening

and there
there will
there will come smudges of spirit
        smudges and dirt and grit
        fallings and darkness of soul
but together
we will weather it together

there will be no status quo
               no normal-is-as-normal-does
We blaze like rebels to be ourselves
        to dance our dance
        to be only the shapes
                     we are inside

and in the unknowing
    in the problem
we will know the One
    to whom all is known
    and by whom all becomes solved

        (even my pain
        even my cries of loneliness and agony
        In the night–
        how they have run away!)
There are no words could turn me
    I know within my soul of souls
    He is right for me
    And the future's clock
            will by its gentle hand
            wash every sob to
            to
            forgetfulness…

Our future will fall into place
        watershed moment by watershed moment.
(Already I see my past strange waiting
                    making sense
    We meet upon the appointed time.

Had it been
a little earlier

and I would not have been right
a little earlier
and your mother may have held you apart
We meet upon the right clock.

Chapter 95
GREG PLANS A PROPOSAL

How to propose?

The helicopter ride brochure lies open before me. I dream of a feast, a table, prepared on some little island, and rushing her off, hearts entwined, in the helicopter, up and up and up. To float the air, to sing our hearts high above the skyscrapers.

Then down down to the feast, to the banquet, to the ring lying in a box, waiting the question that watersheds the Future, that brings us to the new era, the next step....

But I know no one on the Coast–and I would need help to organise and maintain the banquet in readiness....

There had been my suggestion of a theme wedding with knight and princess - and friends as jesters and royalty and monks and Middle Ages fancy dress for all. It had found no common ground.

And I wander her house and garden–I had been given a key–and ponder the hiding of balloons with love messages inside them, lying within the garden and canal edging. Perhaps ....as she comes home, the balloons could hide below the canal wall–and they suddenly are brought up one by one, to be burst and words of love read within our hands as we find our gentle way to the gentle unfurling of the question gently asked...

But the wind would grab and scatter the balloons.

Perhaps inside? But then how to hide the balloons so that suddenly it's the moment.... At dinner, suddenly the touching of hearts and moments of question and answer flooding our memories with newness and change?

Yellow balloons....

That purchase is worth the beginning

And praying quickly, the cheap shop is found and yellow balloons are found. And in the shop, as I look from left to right to back to front, yellow item upon yellow item upon yellow item meet my gaze.

And the basket fills–a changed plan forms...

Another shop for yellow coated licorice and a yellow sauce bottle and some yellow other things. The plan unfolds...

Greg and Kathy Weller

Chapter 96
THE ENGAGEMENT APPROACHES

Time to propose!
He placed things in his rooms
Slowly his apartment became sprinkled with yellow things for the proposal, things which blended in with what was already there. Next to—or inside—the yellow item was a sheet recalling a little of their history together

A yellow writing pad became full with hints about where to look. He had stayed up most of the night placing and tidying and writing and then staggered to bed briefly at dawn

She knew, she planned, to come to dinner in 13 hours. At 6pm he planned they would sit together, have dinner, and then play a treasure hunt game—and at the end, they would enter the back room where a mound of yellow balloons and a caricature of them together, and the words "Marry me" on large laminated paper awaited. As she opened the door, he would tap a song on his tiny tablet, and the speaker in the room would play the best romantic song.

All that was left was to blow up the twenty balloons
… but Sleep pulled his feet to bed

****

You have led my feet to dancing,
my heart has learned to sing

Chapter 97
CHANGED PLANS

He plans dinner tonight. But my back and mind stand as boxers. My body and mind yammer and snarl and overpower.

They overpower…

And I stretch a long tenuous hand to a suddenly weaker tenuous future.

I dial.

He awakened to her call.

She: My back is in agony. I have cancelled work today. Can we cancel our meal tonight? I can't handle the stairs up to your home.

O renew my back, O God.
Flee away the black-clad figures of doubt that would assail my mind.
Rise me up when and how you will.

He: That's no problem, dear dear girl. Um… Hey, could I come to your place today and prep for our meal there. It will take four hours–all I ask is that you don't come out of the bedroom–even to the toilet–without getting permission from me–for the four hours.

She: Sounds exciting!

And he up and undid and unpacked and gathered–and to her house to begin, to hide and plan–and to sneak into the back room, just next her room, and carefully build the mound and the balloons and arrange the art and the proposal and the speakers gently, quietly.

I lie in my bedroom with rose-colour and impatience. He paces and walks and rustles outside for six hours.

How can one walk for six hours an eye-dropper of an apartment? Two bedrooms, a living area, a door…

But he moves for six hours. What does he do as the sun creeps slowly into the afternoon's curtains? What does he do?

He finished a half hour before the meal was to start.

****

You have created fire within my world.
You dance my pulse and joy!

Chapter 98
THE ASKING

Greg announced that all was ready. And she came out excitedly and curiously–looking to see how the apartment had transformed. She looked at normality, she looked at roofing, she looked at life and meal and two dvds.

How, how has he walked these six hours? Nothing has changed.

He works slower than I, but six hours have fled our day and the sun splashes orange on the dimming sky.

And they start the meal and finish the meal in a normal apartment. Her eyes see the everyday, the common, the functional.

I tease: "In these six hours, what has changed. With your hands, what has been placed, has been built, has been done?"

And it becomes time, time for the asking.

And the pad and the telling and the love notes of historical memories *and my world changes* wrapped in a yellow chain *how was that in so clearly my world and and yet not there* or under a yellow sponge on the sink or in a cylinder of yellow thickshake straws *your loving eyes, your sunshine eyes* or under the yellow beach towel *how the room flowers yellow and words–my favourite colour not seen at all during all the evening meal (how seen, how unseen)* or in the Tupperware container of liquorice covered with yellow candy *my favourite colour* lining the edges of shelf and sink and cabinet and glass, and inside each yellow thing, a yellow note *holding the permanence of all our moments together, holding the permanence of our hearts and God.*

Then, the following the pad's directions to find a yellow purse containing the words "Will you..." and to the next pad entry with the words "please go into the spare bedroom."

And she opening the door, *the yellow tablecloth splashed with our caricature and my heart flees* and the music bursting from the speaker, and the words there *marry me?* and the ring on display, *and the words, the words, the words as water to dry ground,* and he on his knees on his knees with love and longing and beating heart and love and anxious palms.

And she yes and the holding and he taking the ring, *gold and three tier, gold and three tier and perfect,* and holding her hand and the ring to her finger–touching every romantic movie each had ever seen and that he had rehearsed and practiced so many times in his head

And the ring to her finger

The ring to her finger

The round seal of love on her hand–the two gold swirls above and below the central diamond–touching their longing that they revolve around God as centre. *O God, our centre, ever always our centre.* The ring even the shape she had dreamed about all the years, was now on her hand, giving her new life. *My love my love, we are two as one ... one ring, one circle, one forever.*

I had dreamed of this all my life, <u>this</u> shape, these tiers. And he says simply, "It was the first ring I saw in the first shop I went into"

And I: I do, I do. And the tears flow down. I am in these tears, my love; I am in these tears for joy, I am in these tears and sunlight, so much sunlight.

And the rush to the parents' house and the showing and the smiles, he so tired, and the ringing of her friends *my friends, my dearest friends, thank you–you held me through the unfinding these many years,* all these many years, and the celebration, and he sinking to a chair *this day is real, this impossible-never-to-come-day is real,* and the excitement and photos of the rings texted and he with bones so tired and all the energy fleeing his bones, and the laughter and fun and planning with her aunts and friends, and he quietly hovering on the precipice of sleep and

…oh, my love, my love, my dearest love! My man, whilst I looked into your eyes as you on one knee bent to put the ring on my hand, the clouds danced like white pebbles the sky, the sun rose, the storm clouds found their corners. I hold you and know life has changed forever. The sun lives here, chasing away the 48 years of pain and sorrow and hurt and depression and brokenness. So many times I had tried to take me to the other Shore, swallowing despair and the fleeing and the unknowing and the leaving…

…now gone.
It is gone, there is no leaving, there is no sunset song, there are no blood-reds at sunset. There is your hand, there is the impossible, there is a God-gift after Jesus, there is you.
There is no map, there is only joy.
There are no words, they are only joy.
There is no despair or hole, there is only hope.

>   *And to you who do it alone,*
>   *to you who know not a right one,*
>   *to you who the years behind stretch,*
>   *and flee away in pain,*

>   *hold on.*

>   *There is hope.*
>   *There is breathing.*
>   *There is possibility.*

I thought I would have doubts,
    thought I would have questions and fears,
But I knew,
    I just knew—
    I just knew—I could see through,
    see through him as years, could
    see our many years.

Greg and Kathy Weller

And while there had been days I couldn't move,
there had been days I couldn't get out of bed
(the fire, the agony of back),
he had been so faithfully there,
making coffee,
putting the liniment on my back,
making sure I was OK,
                 loving me,
                   caring for me,
      in the hardest times,
        in the hardest times with agony and pain,
And it was then I knew he was the right one,
        the right one for me.

And I pray now

        I pray
        I pray that
            I will always be the right one
                   for him as well

Chapter 99
THE TWO SING TOGETHER

I look at your hand in mine,
>So small and cute and hot,
>And I know–
>I know you will not use a net of words–
>>Nor web of words–
>>To mechanise me,
>>To bring me to be
>>>Some lost robot.

I look in your eyes,
>And smell your smell
>And hear your heart
>And I know you will not use your arm,
>>Nor ever your fist,
>>To mechanise me,
>>To bring me to be
>>>Some lost robot.

Together to be,
>to be fully human,
>to be fully transparent,
>to be fully vulnerable to the heart,
>>That beats, right now,
>>Right here, beside me.

Chapter 100
ONLY GOD

God owns us. There is no us that is not given us by God.
He is the air that we breathe
We lean into God first in prayer and commitment...
He is first.

There is never the two of us.

There is always the three of us. There is no destroying of the other here, because the God who is present counsels us to peace and giving and seeing the other as priority to receive the sweeter thing, the choicer gift. Rather than one resting, we urge the other to rest as we take the burden.

We lean into God first, then each other. We enmesh in God first then each other.

Then we us two become his art, his sculpture, his perfume.

I smell your soul perfume–it is beautiful because of Him!

Each incomplete, we interlock perfectly–completely–in God.

Chapter 101
KATHY IS STARTLED BY THE QUESTION FROM GREG AS TO WHETHER SHE LOVES HIM

How can you ask?

We had three hours ago a symphony of souls, deeply joyed together, looked into each other's eyes and....

... now you ask is everything okay?

Do you not remember?

Do you not remember our deep moments in each holding the other's hands, the long gazing in the other's eyes, the laughing together....

Those moments that stretched beautiful gold across our skies...

Do you not remember?

Have your years of fear and rejection run so deep?

Chapter 102
LOVE SONG

Your warmth is amazing
Your warmth is swimming.
Your warmth is something that I reach and touch.

You are so beautiful. You are sunshine that touches my breathing and cheek. You are carnival and fiesta. You make me inhabit sunlight.

I am blinded by you. I am entranced. You weave yellow and delight into this new day.

****

Kiss me gently with all your love
I'll waltz you gently with all of mine
Keep us adoring always our God above
And then in Him how our love does shine

Forever dancing with you in my heart
My embraceable girl, my other breath

Chapter 103
TEARS TO HEAVEN

Tears flow upward to the God who sees and steers, and who dreams of, and is easily capable of, surpassing the realistic best we think He has for us. He has time, has had eternity, to build all His extravagance and His yearning into the future he calls us to walk with Him.

There was never any price—except conscious resolution to see Jesus as the proactive extravagant action by God to make us blameless before God—that Jesus died because death was what we deserved for our ancestors choosing to be permanently inculcated with a hereditary disease within emotion and spirit. Jesus (amazing God) frees you from this virus's penalty and slowly releases you from the virus symptoms.

****

The night feels gently wild
I'm here with your smile
Holding me

Greg and Kathy Weller

The moonlight in your hair
I could stand here
Forever would you mind?

Chapter 104
THE TWO MEET TO SKYPE THE MARRIAGE MAKER

We step out together
   The sun too hot and prickly
   At 8 am
   The sea too sparkly and vast
   near our feet

We skype the friend
   The pastor friend

And we chat
   We talk about breath and breathing
   We talk about the news not believing
                It was true
                (It couldn't be true)

And then we turn
   Turn to the business at hand.
The pastor friend speaks
   "Now, about November..."
And we restless
"Now, about November,
the engagement party..."
And Kathy
   there beside me
   Kathy speaks
And I know
   what she will say...
Kathy speaks
   "Rev, about that..."

                ****

                And I, your princess, watch
                You send the day sun to bed -

Greg and Kathy Weller

                But you stay here, dear sun,
                As I lose myself briefly in your arms
                Pure and waiting and kissing again.

                And I am your sweet temptress, dear man
                Your keeper of the night heated flame.

My heart skips a beat
The joy of last night will repeat
Soon I hold you, take your hand
Taste your lips, embrace your heat

Poetically Together

HUMANS

IN

STACCATO

AND

BLUR

Greg and Kathy Weller

Chapter 105
STACCATO AND SURPRISE

She: We decided
A squeeze of hands under the table
He: We were thinking of the engagement in November, but...
Knees touch, out of sight
...it was just too long. We were planning to get married next year–the weekend just after Easter–that way we always celebrate the death of Christ with the death of hope, and the absolute surprise and joy three days after his death. Then the NEXT weekend, celebrate how we who had no hope and had given up finding someone to love...
The Rev's face on Skype, listening, listening.
...and then the amazement of joy at finding someone. First God, then us two.
She: But to wait 6 months, back and forward between Greg's home and here. Six months–it wasn't going to work.
A Squeeze of hands. The crunch was near.
She: And I was talking to a good good friend, telling them our difficulty, the dilemma. Something she said–it just clicked!
A look at each other.
She: We were thinking of announcing the engagement in November and getting married in April.
The Rev: Yes. Just as we worked out, yes. And we'll be up there for the engagement party.
He: Clearing his throat but not speaking
She: Hey Rev, about that. We decided...
A last touch, tasting love and courage and change
She: The engagement party won't be an engagement... It'll be...
A pause in the air between them
She: We want it to be a surprise wedding

****

> Your hand in mine, your body on my mind
> Your kiss upon my lips, your taste upon my mouth.
> The promise of so still waited for...

Chapter 106
STACCATO AND RUSH

See, my friend and I were looking at how expensive it all was–the engagement, the travel, the wedding months later in April. And she said, why not combine the two: the engagement and wedding? And I thought: what a great idea. I texted Greg immediately to ask...

He: It solved so many problems. Excellent.

You are so close my love. Your hand in mine, hope near hope. Our warmth entwines.

The Rev sat a startled long silence. Words and plans scattered on the floor. "But I thought that November would be the engagement."

"Oh, that's still true"

They smile

"We want an engagement party–for 15 minutes. Then there'll be an announcement that everyone is to meet in the park on the beach in half an hour for our wedding..."

****

> O God our God, our hands in yours
> and then each other's. Our skin and
> fire, our breath and hearts–to you–
> then to the other.

Chapter 107
THE FINER DETAILS

The two sprawled her couch, planning

She: I've found beautiful bridesmaid dresses on the Internet. Brightest yellow, so beautiful.

He: So good! Should we have a bridal waltz?

She was unsure.

He: I know. A surprise dance! We get dressed up and we enter the reception room with a surprise dance.

She: I love it, love it

He; We have to get lessons ... very very quickly

She. My cousin used to be a dance teacher. Let's get her!

The jigsaw was forming
She: We can get Pete to do the photos
He: I don't know. Is he good? After all, these are our showpieces for years to all our visitors and friends, photos on the wall... They are forever.
She: Let's go and visit. He has canvases of his photographs on the wall. And he is good.

****

    You are energy and wine
    Your soul rich and heavy
    You are invigorating and
    So whole and wholesome
    You are everything good and everything hot.

    You are sultry and steam
    You pulse into the corners of my life

Chapter 108
SHOOT

The sun and surf danced together with love. The two hovered near the beach trees at Burleigh.
Pete: ...closer. Rest your arm in the branch
... and he did, feeling wrong
Pete (to her): Now, come in closer, your hands only near his, not touching
.... and she did, feeling her back whisper
Pete : Now turn slightly. No, too much. Back, and back ...and hold.
Click
Pete: Now perhaps over here...
And birds hugged the sun singing in trees. The world drifted past–of no real importance
Position–and click.
Laugh and promise in our looks, our glances.
The reels of the photo carries the promise of our hope.

Chapter 109
CHANGE AND GOD

She was tears, the phone in her hand. "Yes, I understand. Of course. Please, get well soon. We will find someone else."
And then disconnection. The turning
"It's so sad. Our hairdresser… She's not well. She won't be able to do my hair for the wedding. Babe, let's pray."
The coming together; the urgent prayer. Arms around each other, words to heaven
Within ten minutes, a substitute found
We kiss, lean into each other's soul, and marvel in the riches of the transparency of the moment…
…and pray, her friend to health and God

Chapter 110
BUYING A BED pt 1

He, on the phone, feeling his way to phrasing: I had heard–and perhaps it's wrong–that when you're buying a bed, it's good to lie on it for a while to find out if it's going to work. So I was wondering if we could come down and perhaps lie in different beds for perhaps 2 minutes each bed?
The voice: No, no, that won't do at all
He: Oh
The voice: You need at least 10 minutes per bed.
He: Oh that works. Ten minutes per bed. We'll slowly work our way around…
The voice: How about something like–you lie on a range of beds very briefly. Once you've found three likely candidates, lie on each one for 10 minutes?
He: If you're happy with that?
The voice: Absolutely
He: Thanks. Good-bye
The voice: You'll find something great. Good-bye.

Chapter 111
BUYING A BED pt 2

We arrive
Beds—rows and swirls around us. Suites and opulence nestled near walls; functional displays demand the middle of the room.
We drift and chuckle, giggle and dream, from bed to bed, hope to hope, future to lifetime.
Too hard, too small. Skip the one resembling a drawbridge
We find our three...
We lie on each, eyes touching eyes.
Hope and call of our bodies. Decorum and distance. But our eyes speak their speech.
There was a choice made
A king-size bed, half price
Reserved, paid for, settled.
Your kisses are like wine.
The wet of your lips
like nectar on flowers.
I lie beside you, not touching—waiting.
Six weeks! Six weeks!

Chapter 112
THE TWO FEAR THE DRIFT APART

Please please
    don't let us stand
    in years to come
Back to back
    yet untouching...

We step away from
    each other
In repugnance
    refusing
    declaring that even as we stand together

   back to back
Our backs will <u>not</u> touch

And we look away
   never to each other
   We look away

Not seeing the other
   lest we turn
       turn and
   hurl pain at each other
   fire splattering the walls
   (Oh, how hurting people hurt)

No, we stand
Back to back
Miles apart
Our eyes searching
As we untouching
Look backward

Backward

Backward
At the bad choice
The evil bended knee
The
The words that hung in the air
The
    time of the
      mistake.

The mistake and acceptance

(This is our fear)

Then I look for your eyes

And fears meltaway
          cascade away

I hold you as sun
I hear your voice
And
Today scintillates and sparkles
And all the dark fears
          just

       just
       runaway.

Chapter 113
RIPPLES AND RUSHES 1

The pre-marriage counsellor sat, blonde and smiles. "I think a plan is to have special days reserved—one day of the week for romantic dates and another day for sexual intimacy and another day for deep communication."

Deep communication–such as the three questions. Yes, that would work.

"Otherwise life often takes you away from these and each other."

My joy speaks ever of you, my love. I cherish forever your hand and breath. This waiting–such waiting!–it beats painfully against my longing heart.

And into her back: cortisone as a needle, a grand ship into her spine, promising healing or emptiness, springsong or winterburn.

The unmoving…

For two days, the unmoving…

Waiting coiled around clocks, a sheer serenade of ache and longing.

The Travel Consultant poured information and places into his ear. North to Cairns? South and stopping at Perth?

He: Yes, the cruise to Cairns. Ocean and tropics sits well. The ocean surrounded by love.

How soon, how soon, till then, our together leaving? How long, how long–until the I do's and life begins as one? Bring it now! Bring it today!

The counsellor: When you face differences, listen to the other, listen to them present their case, their difficulty. Ask any questions to understand their thoughts. Then go away and think through the validity–will you change; will you not; was it misunderstanding; is it too key to you to change?

She: Yes, so frequently the miscommunication.

"And decide if you will change. If not, then let them know, and they can process...."

But everything with love, everything with adoration to the other. And forgiveness seventy times seven times.

How soon, how soon, other breath? Our kisses long to find their moment...

Beautiful woman, he writes with joy, I have booked our honeymoon. We cruise the fifth of November till the twelfth from Brisbane to Cairns. The motel is booked, the cruise is booked. The travel agent has laboured. We leave the fifth!

My Darling, she writes, puzzled, are we having the honeymoon before the wedding, softly keeping her counsel to herself and her God

He: She is mistaken, she is so wrong. But I don't want to hurt her. If I were to say that she is wrong, that would give hurt, and so I will say nothing and be silent, for I want to never hurt her.

My love, our fever, our longing! My breathing heart, your singing soul!

Counsellor: And in your life together, there is a need for roles, rooted in reality, love, truth and skills. Let's discuss those roles so that they are flexible–but there for when the demands of life come.

My love, you reach for my hand: you caress my soul. You reach to brush my cheek: you are angels' wings beating upon my delight.

The phone crackles and sends his words: "After the wedding on 28th October, there's a week before we have to be in Brisbane for the cruise to Cairns, so I was thinking…"

Her voice back through wires: "But the wedding is the 28th November."

He: November? I've booked the cruise for the first week in November.... But we're not...

She: I was wondering…

He: I… Oh…

Sing, my heart! Though human and often mistaken, we watch the ticking minutes skipping away. May close bodies build passion and be foreverly forever!

His hand upon the phone: Hi? Flight Centre? Yes, about the Cairns cruise–thank you for all the work. It was brilliant! Excellent! I just had the problem that… I had the date wrong.

The other end of the line clicked the disconnect.

He looked at the idle phone for a moment, then thought it best to call to rebuild, to re-plan tomorrow. Let the agent calm first. (He really HAD done a lot of work on the planning and bookings.)

Counsellor: As you go through a difficult time, always remember what made you fall in love with the other one in the first place. Although it can be hard, although it may seem impossible, hold onto that feeling while you work through the issue. And don't be a stranger in that time–but sometimes in action, sometimes in deep communication, sometimes in poetry, sometimes in thanks and kindness, build your love, build each other's heart.

He: To work, to work. A new honeymoon, a new wedding date. Bigger and better! A South Seas cruise from Sydney!

You are hot tonight in my mind. And I here in my unit sit, watch the moon, heart dancing.

The photo booth! And the two, teenagers in older skin, clamber in and poke faces at the camera and roar with laughter. Two, learning to be vulnerable and transparent and holding the hand of the most beautiful present ever found.

You make fever seethe and burn
You steam me up for joy

Two arrived from across the ditch. Mountains of kindness and caring, humour and comedy rippling like the Tasman Sea. Arriving for two weeks in Australia.

Dear, dear friends of Kathy, they came to dinner at her house, and Lloyd and Greg cooked dinner whilst the ladies caught up on the news.

The evening spilled into building scales of laughter. The men studied the recipe, bravely battling theory into the frypan.

Then we all sprawling the chairs on the Gold Coast verandah.

Rosanne: I was in the supermarket and I thought I would bring basmati rice for dinner.

"Who's coming for dinner?"

Rosanne: No, no one. Just us.

"No… Who did you say? Marty Rice?"

Rosanne: Who's Marty Rice?

"Exactly. I invite you to my unit in good faith, and I hear you've roped others into coming along as well

Rosanne: He's here already.

Where?

Rosanne: The rice. It's in the meal.

Oh, do you give all your ingredients names, then? Marty Rice, Tommy Turmeric… Sister Sally Spinach…

And the two ladies beside themselves, laughing.

"Hey, do they go out together–get together and have a nice family casserole in the park?"

Merriment reigned

Rosanne, do you know what Greg texted me this morning? Tell her, baby…

Yeah, sure. It was cold last night at the unit–blanket on, blanket off. Legs outside the blankets, legs back under. So I texted…. Did you find it, Kathy?

Yes… "I have to warmup because I left my legs outside"

Perhaps they were with Marty's family….

Laughter upon laughter.

And another time, "My pillow is hard and my ear is creased"

Greg with broad smile. "OK, how about this…. There's a bright street light near my house, yeah? The other night, I got up to go to the toilet. I was feeling my way to the toilet and was wondering why it was so dark. I was thinking it's always so light and I couldn't work it out. Then I realised…

…I realised I hadn't opened my eyes yet.

"Gregisms we call them. We both love 'em."

Yeah, I can be pretty amazing when I'm half asleep. The other night, I got up from sleep–all I had to do to get to… the toilet… was to walk around a supporting column. So I was half asleep, and thought it would be easy. I put my left foot on the left side of the column. Then I realised my nose was right against the column

Rotfl time.

Sometimes when Greg writes a love note, he tells me I am his best fiancée. So I ask him how many he has!

And on and on.

The evening a ship of joy and memories and friendship celebrated, then farewells and a spilling apart into the evening

We kiss, and there is all our hands and breathing.

We kiss and I count the breathings till I hold you mine

And we two sit in her office *fire* and the Doctor leafs the documentation.

"Unopened tablet boxes as you board the cruise. Now, do you have enough scripts for that?"

And the stillness and peace of the cruise, so honeymoon filled, flees a little at medicines and papers. But the Doctor sits and prints scripts, filling up the PC printer tray. And the handing to us, and the muted taking.

"Have you got enough documentation about your health history?" And pages spill from the printer to our hands.

And the talking of copper bracelets and the price of ship's doctors, ship's medicines, the waiting while sick, the cruise and massages *fire lying* and the last last instructions of massages and knotting.

And we out the surgery, and she her best wishes for our wedding, and our thanking for all she has done over the years–amazing.

And the sitting in the car and regrouping and the unknowing of futures and *fire lying down* determination.

And her tearfulness and vulnerability and her "All of me is all of yours," and the knight inside him rises to protect, to soothe, to solve, to protect–and finds only the unknowing.

And *fire–my lying down* futures envelop the two a moment then slide into corners, and a holding and the unknowing moment passing.

"Wow, wasn't that doctor's visit a lot of paperwork! And to think the ship made it part of the entry requirements!"

"I..." and the finding of lunch, and finding the comfortable seat, the sitting, and the enjoying and the afternoon planning *fire in my–lying down* and the dancing of love in the planning and

Kathy's pondering "Will I get better? How is life to be?" And the rising and the walking-in-hands out, and first steps first *the fire in my–lying down* and the finding of her home, and the finding of knots and the cream rubbed slowly *so much the fire in my back even when lying down* and the whisperings of love while the cream goes on.

Chapter 114
KATHY'S DREAM

He changed one day
He up and rolled through my house
    Like sledgehammers
Running my life into frightened hills and caves.

He up and bought cannonballs
    Whirling them around his heart.
    They would hit me, were I too close
    So I stay away, sit in corners
            small and unwanted

So he turned then and built up the cannon balls
                 on top
                 on top
                 building a wall
I can no longer see him
I can no longer feel him breathing

I can no longer
       Time spurns me
       Time simply carries the years to death
       Time
              after time
                        after disinterested time.

And suddenly I awake
       The damp bedclothes in the summer night
It was a dream

It was only a dream.

Chapter 115
RIPPLES AND RUSHES 2

The four into the car, Kathy driving New Zealanders and Australians to the spit, to the hall, to the chocolate shop. For Kathy, painkillers and her back and chocolate blending into the echo of stories and laughter; her light-headedness as chocolate fought with tranquillizer so that Lloyd drove us home.

And so soon the last drive to the airport. And on the way, even in an obscure alleyway and wholesaler, the New Zealanders found, as always, an acquaintance from their trips around the world. They laughed together and recounted the story of how, when needing to store bags in an airport, and the cloak room undesirable, they had gone to lost property and had said, "We'd like to lose these bags." The clerk had obliged and they had freedom. Then returning to Lost Property, and the returning to them.

Their plane touched cloud and farewells became memories.
And she: My back speaks again hard-edged, speaks again with guns.

Poetically Together

The marriage counsellor: There will be change. You bring your habits and needs and reactions, as do they. You change, you grow. In new times, in sorrow times, in adjustment to how the other responds to your response, you grow. To grow is to embrace potential. And to grow is good because you have learnt bad habits–because you have learnt how your parents solved conflict, you have learnt how you at age 5 sat with disappointment, you have learnt how you at age 13 waited for the unavailable longing or person. You have learnt–now firstly pray, now re-learn, now re-discuss together.

You stand here sultry and breathing, as pending as the too hot coastal nights.

She with sorrow and longing: The wedding dress is too big. It came online and I swim. And the long trip to the seamstress! And their working, their furrowing of brow and the heat of the day... And they much improved–and yes, it works.

The counsellor: And how do you see your life together? As your dreams fulfilled? As change and adventure together? You call yourself the Whirlwind Wellers and smile. Change brings whirlwind–and grace and leaning together in the change. New shared life pours into the transparency and ache and prayer.

And again the back, intolerable and unknowing, unheeding the two's plans.

Wandering the shops, she looking and murmuring, "I like that." And later, "How beautiful." And to a third, "Wonderful. How I adore it!" And looking at him, and his serious face, and "You do know, don't you, dear, that saying I like something is not a request to buy it for me." And he, with smile and relief, "You know, my mum would say 'I like it' and it was code for 'Buy it for my birthday or Christmas or Easter– and I had so thought that you too would.... So, so good," And again the breathing and smile.

And the summer nights and the carnival. And the hands and the laughing. And the longing and dancing of hearts. And the waves roll in passion and song.

He with passion: I am your knight, your servant of the bended knee. My needs I acknowledge but leave till you are safe, till you have had your fill, till you my princess have felt you are princess. I your hero, I your Romeo, I your reacher and finder and strength and heart, so much your heart. *And the sigh and the fire and kiss on parting.*

And they both: God loves and protects and nourishes you, my love, far more effectively than my frail hands and beating pulse and faster breath–now, and this side of time, and in the transition from time, and in the thereafter. I only ask, that in the transition, we plunge by His grace the cold wave together to the forever.

And how much the sitting until the cold hours talking of soul and life and the past and the tears; the loving and pausing of life in the kiss; the clearness of soul as glass revealed; the willingness to nourish–these he brings to her soul in love and these she echoes back in love.

And he: her kiss; her hand on the summer days; her princess eyes finding her knight; her nourishing and her woman's heart.

And we will raise our declarations, our "I do's," on the mountains of God's gift and the valleys of our body's weeping. We vow we will thumb our noses at pain though it come like waiting crocodiles.

And the boardgame bought and the coffee and the sitting in the mall's food court. Hours and laughter and the game and the light in your eyes, the sweet light in your eyes.

How the morning touches the dawn sea with loving hands and promises of day. We push through crisp air and the rapture of souls beneath the sunrise. Then back–and she to work.

And the storm in his head and the need to quietly drive and the hurting and the sorrow… And the need to not let the sun go down on his wrath: to either ponder and resolve, or discuss and resolve. Then sitting and talking together, the earnestness, the knowing of the other's loving will, the adventure and resolution. But how much more often, the earlier solitary prayer and thinking it through and the finding of the resolution without their knowledge.

And sometimes the both, sometimes the pondering, and the discussion.

And he the candy teeth, and she the orange quarter in her mouth, and the showing to the other, and the giggles, and the falling about.

The holding as the sun slides to its rest, and all celebration sings, though fire edges the vocal pain, and a nerve urges her to bed.

And the beginning of a list of dates, taking an internet idea and tweaking the location, or what is held, or changing the energy and chase, or substituting the suggestion for the owned thing. Building the list, and keeping it private–just suggesting one by one as the evenings roll on and on.

And they two to each other: when I know what is right, when I know what you need, when I know your ache and it is in my ability to help, may I never be slow to rush to your side, may I never sin against you by taking my time. May we lean with belief and vigour into God, may we lean with speed and trust into each other. The whirlwind takes my heart to both of you–never as your people pleaser nor my territory claimer, but as lover and nourisher and giver and yielder.

You are always my life, my fiancé, my coming spouse, my singing garden and swansong. How I almost missed you, how I almost didn't send the wink all those four months ago, how I almost walked you by. But you have come with healing–I still find occasionally again the repression and rejection fears, I still march to my imprisonment… But I have come to know your love, and I emerge, a rabbit to his delight, a groundhog to his joy. I emerge, greyness to your yellow, chill chill heart to your warmth.

Poetically Together

And we saw the other day, we saw the story of a man who lost his love, his love who fled and tumbled the night and the box and the transition. And I scare–I would not face life without you. Mortality and our love take the boxer's ring... O God, take us both, take us at once, that neither must find the next day alone.

The counsellor: Set a regular date night, and guard it well, so that neither friends nor overtime nor restiveness nor opportunities take it from you. Keep all work things from your bedroom–that it becomes your pleasure, not your workplace; that it becomes your fire, not the furnace of day's worries recounted; that it becomes your fever and unguarded place. Count your quality hours together each week, and nurture them frequently and well.

The marriage maker: "Try *His Needs, Her Needs*–so so good." *And Greg up and finds the book, and he brings and they two start to read.*

And the octopus and the air rifle and the clowns' heads. And then, ball by ball into clown mouths, the attendant hovering, and the winning of a prize. He had so wanted the large large fluffy cartoon doll, but won the four inch stuffed toy... But she received and held it and smiled, and held even more his heart.

The counsellor: Conflict between you both is an adventure that you and God take together. It can be hell, it can be dark, it can feel like it will take your life. But to listen and negotiate and adjust and pray in your bright burning together and honesty together–to God first, then to each other–brings you to perhaps the point of replacing misconceptions of God or of each other.

Every moment is the adventure that you and God and your spouse walk together: allow it to stretch as long as Abraham's journey if needs; lean into each other so long as you travel, and even more when at rest. Your love is beyond death because God is even there, always there, the ultimate protector and taker of you each and both. Love each other in the giving, love each other without expectation–and then the other loved one echoes love without agenda back into your breath and breathing.

And the street market shows the man in silver sitting as statue and then suddenly to stand, to move his hand, to freeze. And the child blinks and walks up and stretches her hand–the statue holds, the gray clothes and hair. And the statue winks. And the two click their shutters, and he races and photobombs, and they move on, always on.

And she: To love without walls, to love without anything stopping you, is so beautiful because you embrace the freedom and openness of heart and the openness of love.

And he: To be transparent and vulnerable and to know your love: this the freedom and delight and breathing and fire. And I know that if I were to treat you less, to handle your heart with careless or colding hands: that this is wrong, and that God will with vigor correct my sin against you.

And the two sit and dream tomorrows, imagine the dice rolls, the future Christmases and increasing winters, the joys and cheers, the future vibrance and emotions, all that God has done, will have done, is doing and will do.

And they reluctantly stretch their hands to all their mortality and their potential to fall, each and together, as they entangle in their wings and horns. How often the bruised and fading Adam stands as interior sinful and haunting ghost… And they two know that like him they will discover their own large temptation, and in the moment, tumble to fly or falter before its foul breath.

And in some time they know they two will also be the deceased, those entering the kingdom by the skin of His grace, having been both the midnight murderer and God's loving mate, the bad mad liar and the lover of God. And they two look and see there is mud on their toes and grit on their tongues–both now and always, until the forever.

And the two request of families: after marriage, please ring before you come, so that we can be we in the forming, we as one flesh and always becoming so; we are the new learning and communing Adam and Eve each day more truly.

He driving her relative to find his mum, and he: "Yes, I know you can direct me, but I am new to driving in this city, and I need the gps", and the relative "Turn here, turn here!" And he: "But the gps says the next turn" and the chatting–and the eventual arriving.

And the turn, and back to her.

And the outing with her close close friends to the capital, to the fireworks above the water, the "ooh" and the intake of breath, the people crowded on people on people; the late night walk, the fireworks within the good night kiss.

Last plans for the fifteen minute engagement party, and the surprise wedding on the beach, the counting of RSVPs, the anticipation of future and joy of hearts and passion.

And she driving to the airport, and back with the marriage maker and wife, and the long long last-day talks in café's over sliders and coffee. His sliding home to bed, her deep nightlong, nightdeep heart sharing with the marriage-maker's wife. And he waking in the night, and formulating the plan for pouring sands together on the morrow, the wedding-morrow; and she and marriage-maker's wife, wide-eyed on the bed and in the lounge, and in the packing of cases, pouring out hearts and imagining and discussing and solving future wife's problems with her friend, her older so-dear so-dear friend; and he sleeping, exhausted.

And he up, early in the morning! He up, and ringing the marriage maker, and arranging the pouring of the coloured sands, and to packing, to packing. And she sleepless and vibrant, relaxed and joyous, at breakfast with the maker and wife, and to the minutiae, the minutiae.

And he out, deciding to dye his hair black to surprise his heart-surprise, and the stopping to buy a biscuit barrel in the shape of a cow. Hair-colour done and taking the cow home, and the finding of relatives, and the blur and her rush and the speed and the whirlwind--and she standing at the engagement party wondering where he was and singly greeting engagement party guests, and he late, and arriving just in time (two minutes left of the engagement celebration)...

And the calling out by an aunt, and the announcement of invitations to a wedding and date given.

And pause...

And one by one the realisation by guests that it was today, today!

And the two out, she to her dresses and maids, he to the wedding place and to the loudspeakers set up there. And she down the aisle, and he walking to meet her, and they take their place together and breathless and tired and he stressed and she joyous!

And the marriage maker stands among the congregation.

And before the sky and before the sea and before their God, they two stand still to be poured into one flesh.

And before them, there is sand in two cups, his colour in one and hers in the other. And there is a large container, with red sand on its base. And they pour together their sands into the large container to blend and combine and be no longer separate, two souls together as one new flesh; new life, new heart, new sands combined on top of the red, the red sand spread out as Christ, who spreads his life among all who will hear and embrace it in truth.

And the Lord's Supper, they two before the watching crowd. And the book and the pen and the signing as a friend comes to the microphone and sings of hearts and givings...

And the introductions (so newlywed) and the gatherings of audiences and greetings and wishes and smiles and the whisking away for photos and the capturing of hearts and memories, sand and grass and blur...

And the photos and the standing and the glimpsing of clickered shuttered forevers flashing into perpetuity: snapshots of a racing racing day.

And a little back pain.

And the Reception! And the standing at the door to the reception hall, and the breathing and the one—two...

And in, and the so-secretly-rehearsed-but-now-in-public dance to a fifties' song, and the laughing and the cheering in the room, the call of "Encore" and the frantic scrabbling for cameras and phones that it not be missed, the memories not be uncaptured. And the food and the cake and the introductions of newly-mets and...

And under her skin, pain sings as the great performer, so feisty and pointed, kicking at all the conventions and her joy and her life.

And the speeches–speed upon speed, and tiredness upon hurting. Her eyes fade to glass, brittle and breakable.

And the out, the leaving at 9 pm to drive to her place, dire with dying, sliding into slaying with pain, revenge upon her for all those few hours of abandon.

****

Her place, to shower, to pack, to change, to drive to the Sunshine Coast, to the waiting room and sheets--and she departed to the shower, *this pain would disappear me without trace, trickle me to chill and unknowing* he feeling awkward about entering the bathroom and hovers outside *I am totally safe in Christ yet sliding totally into pain* and a call and his rushing in

And she on the shower floor *holding in heart to God and lifepartner* but, but scarce able to speak. And the ambulance *I am a former rebel knowing now my broken body and age* and and the hospital and they two pause in the hall, pause in the hall for hours, stretcher and groom, and she barely barely conscious *I rouse and find him there near me, then fade again near my knight.*

I miss our time on too unordinary an evening.

Pain and I–too strange, too wrong as bedfellows this honeymoon night.

And he numbed standing next her, and wondering…

"Is this an end? Is this an end before beginning? Is this no breath and no future and no hope?"

Pain stands as victor over this my shell, this my unknown unbeing.

"Is it…"

"Do I stand in ashes, and breathe desolation and furnace?"

"And how is it this?"

Stay tuned for the next installment

APPENDIX ONE
THE THREE QUESTIONS

What are the three questions
What have I done this week that made you feel good?
What have I done this week that hurt you?
What is something you would like me to change?

Examples of Greg asking the three questions
(Note:-these following are discussions that did not happen. They are sample question that may be helpful) Two sets of examples are given:-

A sample of what the three questions might be (with a possible response):-
What have I done, my beautiful one, to make you feel good this week?
I really appreciated you helping with the washing up after the meal. It was something we could do quickly. And it set up the evening beautifully because we could just watch the movie without having to worry about the kitchen.

What have I done this week, my love, to hurt you?
When I asked a question the other night, you seemed to snap at me quite harshly.

(It's OK here to ask questions to clarify–but focus on simply clarifying before you go away to prayerfully process your thoughts by yourself. Work on not being defensive in the clarifying. Take the time later by yourself to look at the validity.)

And finally, what is something you'd like me to change?
I've only just started to notice you leave the light on in the toilet, even during the day. Whenever you're aware of it, could you turn the light off when you're finished? It's not a big thing at all, but it might be something that might become an irritation in time.

Another example of the three questions (with responses):-
What have I done, my beautiful one, to make you feel good this week?
I love how every time you see me, you tell me two or three times that you love me. Sometimes after a hard day, that is worth so much more than you could imagine.

What have I done this week, my love, to hurt you?
It hurt me the other day when we were out with a group. I felt like you made a negative comment about me in front of our friends.

And finally, what is something you'd like me to change?
I noticed a couple of times now that there are some drops on the floor in front of the toilet. Is it possible when you go to the toilet, to make sure it's all clean at the end?

Some Tips
- Share the problem and suggest a solution–but stress it's only a suggestion
- When stating the problem, use neutral or gentle verbs which still get the point across, without pressure or putdowns. State the problem using "I feel" or "I find" etc. By using the word "I," you state it is your perception, and this way the other is less likely to feel attacked.
- Allow them to ask questions to gather information from you.
- Allow them the time they need to think about it and make a decision–it could be one minute, it could be two days. But early in your relationship, decide on an agreed upper time limit.
- They have a right to say they can't do what you have asked. If they do, you need to accept it and have a plan if they don't want to change, holding onto the assumption they are still very deeply in love with you and have honestly tried to accommodate your needs, they see them as valid, worthwhile, real, and are trying to be honest and transparent with you.
- If they can't do what you asked, move on with no resentment. If necessary, look for ways you can cope.
- Remember that what you are concerned about may be a family custom/character trait/genetic predisposition.
- If you feel defensive or irritated, say "Thank you. I need some time." Don't continue discussions if not in rational neutrality.
- During your processing time, keep loving them deeply.

Some Thoughts from Kathy about the Three Questions

I remember Greg said in his first email, "Ask me anything". He invited us to dance in transparency and honesty.

But we take great care in asking and answering the three questions... We are Superman telling each other of kryptonite. We are miners telling the other of the deep terror. We are birds that sing of joy and fear. But we are also vulnerable, for in that place we are intimate.

But if there is something which does not impact on the other, if there is something that keeping secret does not impact deep connection to the other, then it is OK to keep it secret.

And there is that which is not necessary to be known (eg past irrelevant history) and we let that live its silence.

And always in this process, love them deeply, promote them deeply.

Offer them always the first choice of your good things, for in that there is love.

Some Thoughts from Greg about the Three Questions

It isn't helpful to raise an issue you've had that day that you have resolved yourself. The unnecessary telling of a departed concern creates a new, totally unnecessary concern in the hearer, and invites the hearer to misread meaning into the situation, springing to an unnecessary hurt (unnecessary because it's been resolved), and to an unnecessary imagining of what they did that could have caused the concern. In their thoughts, they start to ponder, "So you had something of concern … well, what did I do that caused that? What should I change?" It may even stir up anger, fear, anxiety, rage–all due to something that is totally in the imagination, something completely unfounded in reality. And imagination makes us unfree. How hard, how hard it is for the hearer to leave the conversation there, at the point of your saying, "I had something of concern, but its been resolved." without imagining, without seeking the topic and cause of your original concern, to leave the conversation unsaid and to shelve their concern. How hard! How easy to leave their loving, and to play in shadow and confusion... How much a waste of time that could be spent loving each other

Would you like further information about the three questions?

For more detailed information about these three questions, please contact us via our website: gregkathyweller.com

For more information or requests email the publisher at: info@advbooks.com

To purchase additional copies of this book, visit our bookstore website at:
www.advbookstore.com

"we bring dreams to life"™
www.advbookstore.com

www.ingramcontent.com/pod-product-compliance
Lightning Source LLC
Chambersburg PA
CBHW062225080426
42734CB00010B/2026